Series/Number 07-127

SORTING DATA
Collection and Analysis

A. P. M. COXON
University of Essex

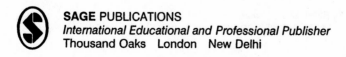

SAGE PUBLICATIONS
International Educational and Professional Publisher
Thousand Oaks   London   New Delhi

For information:

SAGE Publications, Inc.
2455 Teller Road
Thousand Oaks, California 91320
E-mail: order@sagepub.com

SAGE Publications Ltd.
6 Bonhill Street
London EC2A 4PU
United Kingdom

SAGE Publications India Pvt. Ltd.
M-32 Market
Greater Kailash I
New Delhi 110 048 India

Printed in the United States of America

Library of Congress Cataloging-in-Publication Data

Coxon, Anthony Peter Macmillan.
  Sorting data: Collection and analysis / A.P.M. Coxon.
     p. cm. — (A Sage university papers series. Quantitative applications in the social sciences; no. 07-127)
  Includes bibliographical references.
  ISBN 0-8039-7237-7 (pbk.)
     1. Social sciences—Statistical methods. I. Title. II. Series.
HA29.C7744 1999
519.5—dc21   99-17319

99 00 01 02 03 04 05 7 6 5 4 3 2

Acquiring Editor:	C. Deborah Laughton
Editorial Assistant:	Eileen Carr
Production Editor:	Wendy Westgate
Production Assistant:	Nevair Kabakian
Typesetter:	Technical Typesetting Inc.

When citing a university paper, please use the proper form. Remember to cite the Sage University Paper series title and include the paper number. One of the following formats can be adapted (depending on the style manual used):

(1) COXON, A. M. (1999) *Sorting data: Collection and analysis.* Sage University Papers Series on Quantitative Applications in the Social Sciences, 07-127. Thousand Oaks, CA: Sage.

OR

(2) Coxon, A. M. (1999). *Sorting data: Collection and analysis.* (Sage University Papers Series on Quantitative Applications in the Social Sciences, series no. 07-127). Thousand Oaks, CA: Sage.

CONTENTS

Endnotes, References, and Appendices are located on the following website: http:// www.sagepub.com/ shopping/ 407127_Coxon.pdf.

SERIES EDITOR'S INTRODUCTION

The empirical world is a chaos of observation, until we impose an order on it. As social scientists, we select, sort, and categorize, ignoring what we do not want and organizing what we need into data for analysis. The process called "sorting" involves identifying a number of objects and grouping them systematically into smaller categories for study. For example, suppose Professor Ann Jones, a sociologist of work, is examining the occupational structure of an automobile plant and has identified 142 different occupations. She may impose categories of her own, reducing these occupations to six types, e.g., executives, middle management, lower management, crew leaders, skilled workers, and unskilled workers. However, she may have no preconceptions of occupational type or be uncertain about them. In that case, she might ask respondents to sort the occupations into categories, based on their similarity. If she has, say, 10 respondents, she will end up with 10 sorts. The first respondent, R1, may have reduced the occupations to 19 categories, the second respondent, R2, may have grouped them into 2 categories, the third respondent, R3, may have formed 8 categories, and so on. The task of Dr. Jones is to make sense of these sortings, arriving at a classification of occupations in the automobile plant that is, hopefully, mutually exclusive and theoretically meaningful. This example reveals one of the strong appeals of sorting methodology: useful patterns that the researcher had not conceived of might be discovered.

The monograph of Dr. Coxon fully explains how to collect, describe, compare, and analyze sorting data. With regard to collection, he addresses specification, elaboration, and sampling of the "domain" (what is to be sorted). With regard to the sorting itself, he discusses the criterion, the pretest, administration, and the recording of results. He gives special consideration to handling the problem of "lumpers" (who tend to put all objects into one category) and "splitters" (who tend to put each object into its own unique category). Further, he unfolds a real research example, where respondents in the Coastal

North Carolina Socio-Economic Study were first asked to describe the contents of three domains, including Qualities of the Area, Uses of the Environment, and Perceptions of Change. For description of a sorting, he especially offers the height measure, which assesses "lumpiness." Of course, it is useful to compare sortings across individuals. The sortings of two subjects can be compared through their "overlap," as defined in an "intersection matrix." To illustrate a comparison of many subjects and their sorting, real data from the Occupational Cognition Project are provided.

Once the sorting data are gathered and reviewed, the researcher commonly moves on to analysis questions, perhaps about the general data structure or individual differences in sorting choices. For example, to represent sortings data, Dr. Coxon explicates spatial models, such as multidimensional scaling or correspondence analysis (in the series, see also, respectively, Kruskal and Wish, No. 11, Weller and Romney, No. 75, and Clausen, No. 121), and discrete models, such as cluster analysis or tree analysis (in the series, see also, respectively, Aldenderfer and Blashfield, No. 44, Bailey, No. 102; and Corter, No. 112). At present, no one computer software package exists to cover every need for sortings data collection and analysis. Happily, an appendix extensively details the available softwear, its capacities and location. Taken together, the elements of Professor Coxon's monograph make it the most complete handbook around on data sorting techniques.

—*Michael S. Lewis-Beck*
Series Editor

SORTING DATA
Collection and Analysis

A. P. M. COXON
University of Essex

1. INTRODUCTION

There is nothing more basic to thought and language than our sense of similarity; our sorting of things into kinds.

Quine (1969, p. 116)

Categorization and classification—putting a number of things into a smaller number of groups and being able to give the rule by which such allocation is made—are probably the most fundamental operations in thinking and language and are central to a wide variety of disciplines. In a social science context, the process of a person performing such an allocation is called the method of sorting, and the outcome is the most common scale of all, the nominal scale.

In one guise or another, categorization by sorting objects into piles has been commonly used in a variety of cognitive and social sciences especially since the 1950s—the earliest reference is probably a facial-expression sorting study (Hulin and Katz, 1935). As a method, it is known under different names. Substantively, psychologists tend to refer to subjective classification (Miller, 1967, 1969; Imai and Garner, 1968) and subjective categorization (Bruner, et al., 1956) or "partonomy" (Tversky and Hemenway, 1984), anthropologists refer to folk taxonomy (Berlin et al., 1968), and sociologists and social psychologists refer to social categories and social classifications (Hubert and Levin, 1975; Coxon et al., 1986). Implicitly, sorting methods are also used to define library classification systems, medical diagnostic tools, botanical nomenclature systems, and occupational classifications.

Viewed as a method of data collection, methodologists have also used a range of names for the sorting technique; the most general common term is "sorting" (whether free/unconstrained or fixed/constrained in the number of categories used), but it is also known in

1

attitude theory as "own categories" (Sherif and Sherif, 1967), in cognitive anthropology as "pile-sorts" or "stacks" (Weller and Romney, 1988; Trotter, 1991), as well as "clustering" (Fillenbaum and Rapoport, 1972), "free-grouping" (Stringer, 1967), and "subjective grouping" (Rao and Katz, 1971). Mathematicians and statisticians refer to the resulting set of categories as a "partition" of the set of objects (Arabie and Boorman, 1973; Day, 1981). In this text the term "partition" refers to the mathematical structure: the set of disjoint subsets of a set of elements, whereas "sorting" refers to the actual empirical division of the domain-set into nonoverlapping subgroups, whether by the subject as a data-collection task or as a "given" of the categorization.

There is nothing in the method of sorting that restricts it to being simply a systematic method of data collection, using subjects to create categories or "piles of objects" in a sorting "experiment"; the sorting or partition can just as easily have arisen as a result of purely natural or nonreactive processes (such as the presence of artifacts in a set of graves). Nonetheless, the main focus has been in the area of data collection—primarily in anthropology and psychology—where it is used both as an eliciting tool for "folk taxonomies" and as a way to infer the subjects' covert culture (Black, 1963). She cogently describes the purpose as follows:

> The aim is to elicit data which give native classifications of phenomena, how people perceive their environment, what they attend to when making discriminations between classes of things and events; to get descriptive categories which are 'psychologically real,' significances and 'meanings' based on informants' inferences rather than investigators'; in short a discovery procedure which *discovers* not just observables from which to infer, but a meta-level of cultural communication—the inferential relations that members of a given society commonly share about the things *they select* to observe (Black, 1963, p. 1348; emphasis in original).

The method of free-sorting has several obvious and immediate advantages:

- It is not a taxing technique and corresponds closely to natural mental activities; moreover, subjects usually enjoy it.

- It can readily be used in nonliterate cultures and contexts by using pictorial representations of the objects; it has also been used with children as young as three and four (Russell and Bullock, 1985; Best and Ornstein, 1986).
- It can easily be used with a large number of objects: sets of 120 objects are by no means uncommon, and the whole operation takes relatively little time.

The basic operation of sorting consists of subjects allocating a set of objects into categories of their own choosing (although in the case of some sortings, the category system already exists). The researcher usually defines a common set of "objects" (stimuli, statements, names, artifacts, pictures) and then typically asks each of the n subjects to:

> *sort* the *p objects* into a subject-chosen number (c) of *groups / categories*.

Each sorting is done according to some criterion (such as "general similarity"), which is either specified by the researcher or chosen by the subject. As a matter of terminology, "objects" are equivalently referred to as elements, cards, or stimuli and "groups" are referred to as categories, clusters, or piles.

The equivalent mathematical representation of the sorting is:

> the *partition* of a set of *p elements* into a number (c) of *cells*.

The most important characteristic of a partition is that the categories of a subject's sorting must be mutually exclusive and exhaustive, i.e., each object must be sorted into one, and only one, category. This allows an object to be put into a category by itself (often called a "singleton"), but it explicitly disallows overlapping categories.[1] This characteristic of "disjoint categories" is also the defining characteristic of Stevens' "nominal scale" (Stevens, 1959), and so sorting data are (at least initially) at the nominal level of measurement.

Sorting data usually arise by the respondent placing the set of "objects" (usually, cards containing the name or picture of the object) one by one on a table, forming piles, which become the categories. But such data can also arise by some naturally occurring division of the domain of interest. For example, an ethnographer studies how a set of drug users ("objects") foregather on a given night in a number of sites (categories) in a city, or a sociologist compares two different schemes of occupational classification (partitions) by seeing how the same set of occupational titles (objects) is allocated to the social class categories of each scheme. From the point of view of analysis, it is methodologically irrelevant whether the data are elicited as a task for the subject or are naturally occurring, although the former is the more common state of affairs in the social sciences.

In this book, the paradigm of sorting is the *disjoint free-sorting*, where a fixed set of objects are allocated to an unspecified number of categories, but each object is allocated to only one category. But other special cases of sorting are covered, such as fixed-sorting, overlapping sorting, merging, and hierarchy construction, and they are treated in Section 2.6.2 below.

1.1. Measurement, Data, and Sorting

In discussing sorting data in this general way, it is important to make some methodological principles clear. The important and liberating "theory of data" developed by Coombs (1964) and his successors[2] begins by making a crucial distinction between "observations" (in effect, the raw material of data, as normally understood; what Coombs himself also calls "recorded behavior") and "data" (these same observations *interpreted* and *selected* in a particular way). In so doing he emphasizes that the researcher is necessarily involved in a selective and creative role in deciding what aspects of observations are to be represented as data and what assumptions are to be made about them ("we buy information with assumptions—facts are inferences, and so also are data and measurement and scales," as Coombs famously states, 1964, p. 5). One important consequence of this approach is that there can be no such thing as "the (one) appropriate method" for analyzing observations, however strong the conventions existing in the methodological community may be. Yet more importantly, Coombs concludes *"there is no necessary interpretation of any behavioral example as some particular kind of data"* (1964, p. 6; emphasis in original), and we are therefore committed both to a form of methodological pluralism and also to the practical advisability of using several forms of analysis on the same data.

The Coombsian perspective has considerable consequences for explaining and analyzing sorting data. The method of sorting produces "behavioral observations," which give information about details of category membership, e.g., what group an object is allocated to. How this allocation has arisen is irrelevant from the point of view of the theory of data. Usually it would have been produced by asking one or more human subjects to perform the sorting task according to a set of interviewer-provided instructions. But the allocation might equally well have been a categorization produced by some naturally occurring process, as in the sociobiological example of sleeping groups of vervet monkeys studied by Struhsaker (1967) over a 6-month period: "nearly every evening, just before sunset ... the vervet groups divided into sleeping subgroups that spent the night separated from one another by at least one impassable break in the tree-canopy"[3]—and each night's observation can be considered as a separate sorting. So while the prototypical case of the method of sorting for social scientists might be the interviewer-instructed task, there is no reason why different forms of allocation should not be considered as equally valid sortings: anything that partitions a finite set of objects into distinct groups is eligible to be studied by this method.

Moreover, researchers will also show selectivity in concentrating either on representing individual differences in sorting or on the pattern of difference between the objects themselves, aggregated over the individuals' data—or indeed, in looking at both. And depending on their decision, different forms of analysis will be appropriate and will need to be explained. The answer to the question of "what do I do with this information once I have collected it?" is therefore going to depend in large part on decisions already made and on what assumptions the researcher wishes to bring to interpreting the observations. Having interpreted to sorting observations as a given type of data, the class of appropriate methods for those data now becomes more restricted and easier to choose.

Finally, a point about the "level of measurement" of sorting data. In its basic form, sorting is designed to produce a set of mutually exclusive and exhaustive categories. This makes it most naturally interpretable as a nominal scale, since it satisfies exactly the criterion for that scale type: that it be a partition of the set of objects. The researcher may decide to go no further than that and choose methods of description and analysis which make no further assumptions.

These so-called "combinatorial methods" (Arabie and Hubert, 1992) are little known and will form a major focus for analysis in this text. But equally, other researchers will wish to quantify such data and derive inferences about order and distance information in the data. This, too, is a perfectly legitimate aim, and the scaling and clustering procedures designed to extract such information will form another main focus for the book.

1.2. Examples of Sorting

The following brief examples of both naturally occurring and elicited sorting partitions show that a little ingenuity is sometimes called for in considering what counts as a category and what counts as an object, but equally the examples demonstrate that the range and type of applications of the sorting technique are extensive. (More detailed examples are given in Table 4.)

General instances include:

- diagnosis: allocating a set of patients (objects) into a diagnostic classification (categories)
- bibliography: allocating a set of book titles (objects) to a bibliographic classification system (categories)
- thematic analysis: identifying a set of coded themes (objects) present in a set of open-ended interview schedules (categories)

Specific examples include:

- content analysis: of a set of themes (objects) present in a set of newspaper editorials (categories) (Schmidt, 1972)
- semantic analysis: of a set of words (objects) sorted into piles (categories) in terms of similarity of meaning or linguistic properties (Steinberg, 1967; Miller, 1967, 1969; Anglin, 1970; Fillenbaum and Rapoport, 1972)
- food: examining the contents (objects) of a household's kitchen cupboards (categories) or ingredients (objects) that go to make meals (Murcott, 1983)
- sensory phenomena: tactile feel (Hollins et al., 1993); odors (Lawless, 1989; MacRae et al., 1990)
- social networks: identifying the cliques among a set of wind-surfers (Freeman et al., 1988)

- sociometrics: observing the co-dormition of a group of monkeys (objects) in a set of trees (categories) (Struhsaker, 1967)
- social categorization: of a set of ethnic groups (objects) sorted into piles (categories) in terms of their overall similarity (Jones and Ashmore, 1973)
- social classification: allocating a set of occupational titles and/or descriptions (objects) into classes/groups (categories) in terms of their structural similarity (Burton, 1972; Coxon and Jones, 1979a)
- social status: allocating a set of Italian families to status groups according to the degree of their *rispetto* (Silverman, 1966)
- levels of comparison: of subjective classification based upon expert versus novice and visual (photograph) and lexical (word names) versions of similarity of fish (Boster and Johnson, 1989)
- inference: of marriage rules in an ethnically mixed context, by sorting photos and descriptions of possible partners according to suitability for dating, marriage, and approval of parents (Nave, 1998)
- health environments: sorting patient names and physical activities into a set of freely chosen clusters to characterize present and desired ward layout (Canter and King, 1996)
- beliefs about disease: the sorting of disease names and descriptions into piles (categories) in terms of "what goes together" (D'Andrade et al., 1972; D'Andrade, 1976)
- dermatology: using photographs of drug users' skin lesions (needle tracks) to produce an expert ranked categorization of types in terms of how consistent lesions are with drug use (Cagle et al., 1998)
- risks: sorting of 43 types of risk by a group of Navaho young men to investigate (pre- and posttest) the effect of an education-intervention program concerning AIDS, alcohol, and drugs (Trotter and Potter, 1993)
- sexual activity: co-occurrence of sexual activities (objects) within a given sexual session (category) in sexual diaries (Coxon, 1996)
- physical/sexual attraction: sorting photographs (objects) into clusters (categories) of desirable physical image type by heterosexuals of female models (Sherman et al., 1997) and by male homosexuals of male models (Coxon, 1996)
- archaeology: identifying the presence of cultural artifacts (objects) within neolithic graves (categories) (Petrie, 1899; Kendall, 1971)[4]

2. COLLECTING FREE-SORTING DATA

All organisms divide objects and events in the environment into separate classes or categories. If they did not, they would die and their species would become extinct. Therefore, categorization is among the most important decision tasks performed by organisms.

Ashby and Maddox (1998, p. 251)

To conduct a free-sorting experiment, it is necessary to have:

- an explicit set of "objects," or things to be sorted (the "domain"),
- an explicit criterion in terms of which the objects are to be sorted,
- a set of instructions, and
- a record sheet, including a data-record.

When used as a method of data collection from human subjects, a typical instance would be to use a (randomized, shuffled) pack of record cards (each with the name of one constituent object on it) that is given to the subject. The instructions might then be to: *"sort these cards into as many or as few groups (or piles) as you wish in terms of [the specified criterion], or which 'naturally go together.' You are free to rearrange, break or remake them until you reach an arrangement which is satisfactory to you."* (This version relies on Miller's (1969, p. 170) injunction to allow rearrangement to maximize reliability.) Usually, subjects are then asked to name and/or talk about the groups they have made, and it is often worth noting the physical arrangement they have made to detect any implicit arrangement, ordering, or hierarchy they may have produced.

2.1. Specifying the Domain

The rationale of sorting as a data-collection process can most easily be explained in terms of the cultural, social, and psychological processes involved. In these terms, the purpose of sorting methods is to analyze a domain of interest by

- examining the ways in which different individuals categorize the domain's constituent instances
- (and possibly eliciting the instances if the domain is especially problematic or ill-defined) and

8

- hopefully deriving the rule(s) in terms of which the allocation of instances is made.

The notion of a "domain" has best been articulated in cultural anthropology and ethnography, where its use principally refers to any coherent conceptual area or bounded territory, and has been defined as: "an organized set of words (or unitary lexemes),[5] ... that jointly refer to a single conceptual sphere, e.g., a systemic culture pattern" (Romney et al., 1986, p. 313).

The sets of words, photos, or objects are usually chosen to represent an area of interest—occupations, vegetables, photographs of facial expressions, reproductions of paintings, nations, names of members of a social group, etc. In some cases (such as classifications of occupations or lists of nation-states) there are preexisting, publicly accessible lists of the objects, and the issue is then only to find some feasible method of sampling or selecting them. This can be more difficult than might be supposed, since such lists are often an ill-specified compromise between the desire for comparability with previous research, to limit the number to be used, and to produce a set that will be representative of the domain in some way. Thus, in the case of occupational titles (Coxon and Jones, 1974), the choice to inherit a list from previous research will already reproduce earlier inherent biases, such as excluding "unsocial" occupations such as prostitute and including particular titles primarily of interest to the grant-awarding authority.

To define the domain, two complementary forms are available: the *intensive* and the *extensive* definition. In logic, an *intensive* definition is used to specify the rule by which an object can be identified as an instance of the domain and is necessary when no listings exist or where the domain is very large or infinite. An *extensive* definition by contrast defines the domain by enumerating all members or instances of it. Ideally, both should be equivalent, but in practice they rarely are. In research practice, the need will be rather for developing a working definition, needing to be modified to take exceptions into account. More typically in social science contexts, the emphasis is upon social or cultural definition: we need to know what the members of a particular culture or subculture *count* as an instance of the domain, and this is often not known in advance and has to be examined empirically. In brief, the constituent objects of a domain often need to be elicited from the subjects concerned.

2.1.1. Methods for Eliciting Contents of Domains

The most efficient and satisfactory way of eliciting the contents of a domain are those used routinely by psycholinguists to elicit the content and aspects of the "subjective lexicon" (Miller, 1969; Fillenbaum and Rapoport, 1972; Anglin, 1970), by anthropologists to define a cultural domain (Black, 1963; Romney and D'Andrade, 1964; Weller and Romney, 1988; Borgatti, 1998), and by qualitative sociologists to elicit a folk taxonomy by use of frame-elicitation (Miles and Huberman, 1994). These techniques may include:

- free-association,
- free-listing,
- (divisive) taxonomy construction, and
- focus groups.

Free-association is used primarily in psychological contexts and is well described by Anglin (1970) and Bousfield et al. (1958). Subjects are given a starting word (often the domain name itself) and are asked to say quickly what first comes into their head (thus "table" will often elicit "chair" from adults, but "eat" from children).[6] A more useful variant of this is recursive concept analysis (RCA) (Kiss, 1966), where the stimulus word can be responded to by several word responses, and each word-associate is used as the starter for the next stage. This generates a network of associates with paths of multiple associations. From the subjects' responses, a lexicon of words—a kind of cultural or social dictionary—is constructed (with the frequency of their citation), providing a starting set for other techniques. Cultural patterning of word association is indicated by the fact that the distribution of the associates of any one work is markedly skew: associates tend to be very frequent indeed or very rare (idiosyncratic).

Free-listing is usually a more useful and productive procedure. As in free-association, the subject is given the name of the domain and then asked to list (write down or say aloud) as many instances or examples as possible. Attention is paid not only to the instances, but also to gaps and connecting phrases that occur in the process of eliciting, such as "... and then there's ...").[7] The reason is that subjects' lists often exhibit categorical structure, with these gaps providing evidence of category boundaries. Free-listing also produces a more extensive lexicon, and some subjects produce an immensely large number of instances, especially if they are interested in the area.[8] For this reason, care must be taken to ensure that the task is not viewed as a knowledge test by the subject, and embarrassing long silences should be avoided.

Taxonomy construction consists of getting the subject to construct a "folk taxonomy"—a conceptual system organized hierarchically (Berlin et al., 1968; Bernard, 1988)—beginning by dividing down the domain and specifying (usually) what "kinds of x" she thinks there are[9] ("... *Occupations? Well there are Professions, skilled workers and unskilled workers ...*"). Then the subject is invited to divide down each of those "kinds of x" in turn ("... *Professions? Two kinds: Old and New ...*") and may decide for any of the branches that it is not further divisible). This process continues until the subject has terminated all of the branches. She is then asked to provide examples or instances of each of the branches. This "top-down" taxonomy procedure complements the other methods by focusing on mapping the domain from the most general to the more particular. The resulting list of instances once again forms a resource for constructing the lexicon, the specification of the domain.

Focus groups consist of a group of individuals with an interest in the domain, who meet to talk out a particular topic in a semistructured way. Used in many forms of pretesting, the idea is to get the participants to articulate views, opinions, and judgments about a domain and generate material from which the researcher can construct components of the lexicon.[10]

2.1.2. Operational Feasibility: How Many Objects?

Having constructed a resource of "objects," a "sampling," of the domain, it is normally necessary to reduce the number somewhat. A frequency-count of the objects will reveal that some objects are almost universally recognized, while others are idiosyncratic or unique, and the preference will normally be to retain the more common objects.[11] Typically, if the objects are reduced to rank-order and charted by their frequency, there will be a highly skew distribution with a long tail of 1s, similar to Zipf's rank-frequency "law" relating the frequency of use of words in a language and their length (Miller and Chomsky, 1963, pp. 456–464). The goal is to retain culturally shared objects of a domain and exclude idiosyncratic ones. Exactly where that division is drawn is to an extent arbitrary, and it is important to include in a single root form the variants and inflexions of a word ("am, is, are, were ...") as well as to decide whether to merge variants at different levels of generality ("horse, colt, foal, pony ..."). Before making a final decision on what objects to include, it is sensible to check on whether there are any obvious omissions and how well (or accurately) each object is recognized. This can best be done at the pretest stage, when the subject can be asked to inspect the objects before beginning the sorting and report any which she is unsure about and (after the sorting operation) report on any objects that are absent. Where appropriate, visual objects such as photographs are preferable to verbal stimuli, especially with children or subjects from nonliterate cultures or where objects are more likely to be recognized pictorially rather than verbally. (Consider the vegetable kohlrabi—many people recognize it without being able to name it.)

The main practical question is: how many objects may feasibly be used? The answer depends upon two linked factors: the method of data collection to be used and the information-processing capability and cognitive strain that the method imposes on the data-provider. Fortunately, the method of sorting is very accommodating compared with other methods of systematic data collection. For pair comparisons, the number of judgments increases approximately as the square and triadic comparisons as the cube of the number of objects. Even with the use of incomplete experimental designs, domain-sets over 12 become unfeasible for these methods. By contrast, object-sets of much greater size are clearly feasible for sorting, and objects in excess of 250 are recorded in the literature [van der Kloot and Slooff (1989) use 281 objects]; sets of around 100 are fairly common, sets of about 40 or so are most common, and sets as small as 5 are recorded (Hojo, 1986).

2.2. The Criterion

The criterion for sorting has different functions depending on the kind of sorting being used. In the case of preexisting sortings (e.g., bibliographic schemes or thematic analysis), the criterion has already been used to produce the partition, and there are few problems. In most cases, however, the subjects are going to be instructed to create a categorization, and the criterion used then becomes crucial. The reason is that if such categorizations are going to be interpreted cognitively—as evidence about how people divide up the social world—then we shall need to match as closely as possible what is known about human categorization and the task which we shall set them. In effect we are treating information about the domain as cultural unknown and are attempting to guess at, and finally characterize, its contents and structure.

The two most basic principles about category formation (Rosch, 1977, 1978) are (1) that they provide maximum information with least cognitive effort and (2) that the perceived world comes as structured information rather than as arbitrary or unpredictable attributes. "Thus maximum information with least cognitive effort is achieved if categories map the perceived world structure as closely as possible ... " (Rosch, 1978, p. 28).

Of particular relevance for empirical studies of categorization are the following findings:

- Categories tend to be defined in terms of *prototypical instances* (central, most typical, *par excellence* instances) that contain the attributes most representative of the category. In the process of collecting data about categorization, it is sensible to ask the subjects which instances they count as prototypical of each category.
- Most human category systems do not have well-defined, clearly delimited boundaries,[12] and techniques for sorting therefore need more emphasis on such "central representatives" than concern about subjects' uncertainty about allocating marginal elements.
- When a context is not specified (say, in a sorting task), people typically contribute their own. It is judicious therefore to enquire about the details of the "normal" context that they are being implicitly asked to assume.
- "Categories group things which share common attributes" (Rosch and Mervis, 1975; Tversky and Hemenway, 1984)—this is an empirical finding, and not just a definitional convention.

The criterion most used to define the process of sorting into piles/categories is that of "similarity"[13] between the elements. It owes its main origin to Miller (1969) who used the term "similarity of *meaning*" since he was dealing with the semantic lexicon and "meaning" is thus the central concern. (Note, incidentally, that he talks of *similarity* of meaning and not *the same* meaning, which would reduce the semantic task to finding synonyms.)

The wording of other general criteria that have been used to aid the subject in making their categorizations include:

- how similar they are/seem to you (or are to each other),
- denote/are considered similar sorts of ...,
- belong together (or, belong in the same category together),
- naturally go together, and,
- cluster together.

Occasionally, *difference* is also added into the criterion (Donderi, 1988, p. 580): "*Sort the stimuli into groups 'so that the [pictures] in each group are alike but that each group is different from the other groups in the way that is most clear to you'.*"

These general criteria refer to similarity, relatedness, or co-occurrence, and although they have been criticized for overgenerality, it is hard to see how else a judgment of overall similarity or category-belongingness can be obtained, especially when the researcher is also interested, as is often the case, in investigating what the grounds of those similarity judgments actually are. To this extent, the method of sorting is rightly referred to primarily as a method of discovery.

2.3. The Pretest

Many applications of sorting neglect the need to pretest it, but it is imperative for its use as a data-collection task if the understanding and interpretation of the task and the data are relevant. The primary aims of the pretest are to be forewarned about shortcomings in the key aspects of the administration and understanding of the sorting task and to assess the feasibility of the methods of recording. This mainly consists of:

1. checking on the subject's understanding (and/or recognition) of the stimuli,

2. enquiring about the grounds of (and the reasons for) the subject's similarity judgments, and

3. assessing the reliability (stability) of the sorting and the ability to produce other sortings on the same criterion.

A small and in some way representative group of subjects is needed to check these aspects. Without explaining the purpose of the task at this stage, the stimuli (usually cards with the name of the object printed on it) should be randomized or shuffled and given to the subject as a pack. He should then be allowed to lay the cards out on a table and pick out any that he does not understand, recognize, or know about. If possible, he should also briefly describe the object named on each card. [This provides information not only on correctness of his definition but also may be relevant to assessing later the salience of the attributes he uses to judge similarity, since this is a key component of an important theory of similarity (Tversky, 1977).] It can sometimes be useful to include a "bogus" stimulus; subjects often happily include fictitious, rare, or easily mistaken examples in their similarity judgments, such as Ruritania among nations (fictitious), or of samphire among vegetables (rare), or an actuator (instead of actuary) among occupations (easily mistaken).

After being given the instructions, the subject can be encouraged to verbalize her allocations and the reasons for her actions, since this will provide evidence not only of the justifications advanced for allocation, but also of difficulties in allocation—e.g., dithering between piles, indicating a marginal or borderline example. It also acts as an important lead-in to the naming of the groups and often gives a more expansive characterization of them.

Assuming a compliant subject, it is often useful to ask her to reproduce or repeat the same sorting to check on reliability by the similarity between the two partitions or to see whether she can spontaneously produce a different sorting on the same, or even different, bases (Rosenberg and Kim, 1975).

2.4. Instructions and Administration of the Task

We now come to the core of data collection in the sorting task: its administration by the researcher. It is assumed that the domain

16

elements have already been decided upon and numbered sequentially for ease of reference.

The simplest and most basic procedure is first described:

1. *The objects*: Each object name is copied to a small index card of a size that is easily sorted or dealt like a pack of playing cards. Each card can be marked for ease of reference with the object number on the back.[14] If an object name is obscure or likely to be mistaken, a definition can also be provided. Before administration, the deck of cards is thoroughly shuffled. This produces a randomization of the objects and ensures that no one object occupies the same position in each administration. This procedure avoids possible biasing effects due to order in presentation, such as primacy and end-effects (where the first and last objects, respectively, in a presentation significantly affect the later judgments).

2. *Instructions*: The subject is handed the deck of cards and is given the chance of looking through them and asking questions about the objects. The task is then explained. Note that:

   • The *criterion* (e.g., "*group them in any way that seems natural to you*") must be part of the instructions, as well as

   • *Specific instructions* about what the subject is expected to do (e.g., "*sort these cards into as many or as few groups (or piles) as you wish in terms of [... the specified criterion ...]. You are free to rearrange, break, or remake them until you reach an arrangement that is satisfactory to you*"). It is best not to alert the subject to producing groups with only one object in it (singletons), but it is perfectly admissible for an object to be considered to share no attributes with any others. However, the singletons must not be put into a separate *group* of "those that do not belong" or "those I know nothing about"; each singleton must feature as a separate, singleton, group.

3. *The task implementation*: If possible, the researcher should monitor and record the process of group formation,[15] and it is important to note what objects form the core of each group, i.e., the very first to be paired. These will often provide information about which objects are prototypical, i.e., best represent the group. The subject should be encouraged to verbalize as he does the task (and the verbalizations should be tape-recorded for possible future transcription). These verbalizations should include not only the subject's account of what he is doing, but also information about the strategy he is using to produce the sorting.

4. *Naming*: Having arrived at a set of piles or groups that the subject is satisfied with, he should be asked (a) to provide a brief name for each (nonsingleton) group and (b) give a short description of it.

5. *Prototype(s)*: Having identified and named a (nonsingleton) group, the subject should then be asked to name one (or more) objects as "the best examples" of the group, i.e., those that best characterize its content. These form another basis for deciding on prototypical instances.

6. *Arrangement*: It is often instructive to see how the subject uses the table-top (two-dimensional) space as he does his sorting. In some instances, conceptual distance may be mirrored in separation between the locations of his groups, and in more rare instances the space becomes unidimensional as the groups are placed in order (linearly). Because the arrangement may have significance for the subject, he may be invited to say whether his groups are in any particular "arrangement" (a term that does not predispose the subject to think of an ordering) and describe what that arrangement is.

7. *Data identification*: Before ending, each pile of cards of the subject's sorting should be marked with the subject's identifier code (and sorting number, if there is to be more than one sorting).

In recent years, computer data-capture has been adapted to sorting tasks. An example of such technology applied to collecting sorting data on auditory stimuli is given in Bonebright (1996). Icons on the left-hand side of the screen were used to represent the objects (sounds), which were produced when clicked on. Sorting groups are formed by the subject dragging the icon to the right-hand side of the screen and forming "piles" in column positions. Subjects checked their allocation by listening to the noise icons in each column/group and, as in the usual case, they were allowed to reallocate them where necessary to arrive at a satisfactory sorting. A version of "drag and drop" pile-sorting is also provided in the CONCEPT-SYSTEMS package (Trochim, 1989; see Appendix 4 on website).

It is also possible to adopt the sorting task to the questionnaire context. The objects can be listed (and numbered) on the left-hand side of the page, and a number of boxes (representing piles or categories) can be drawn on the right-hand side. Respondents are then asked to assign objects to a group by writing its reference number in the box concerned. Clearly, the instructions have to be perfectly explicit about what is required, especially in the case of the self-administered questionnaire. Boxes can be labeled alphabetically, and respondents can be asked to name them. The layout of such a task in a questionnaire probably restricts the feasible number of boxes (for free-sorting), and it is often preferable in this context to specify a fixed number. In any event, the sorting task is certainly adaptable to interview and self-administered questionnaire contexts.

2.5. Data-Recording

At the end of a sorting, the task should be written up in the form of an interviewer's record. The purpose of the report is to document observations and information about the sorting, and record the data in an format (the PDF—preferred data format), which will make it acceptable to a majority of computer programs designed for their analysis.[16]

Preferred data format (PDF) is a particularly compact and software-friendly way of presenting the data. For sorting data, the PDF consists of having a row vector for each respondent, containing as many column positions as there are objects. It is assumed that the subject's groups or categories have been numbered sequentially, and although the number given to the group/category is entirely arbitrary, it is sensible to number the groups in the same order as they were collected. The entry in the individual's row vector specifies the category/group number in which the object is located.

A simple example of three sortings and their encoding in basic format and in PDF is contained in Table 1.

2.6. Variants of Free-Sorting

The main variations in free-sorting occur principally with respect to (1) the objects and (2) the sorting procedure.

2.6.1. Variations Based on Objects

The usual form of the object is a card with the name of the object on it. Obvious variants of the written card include

1. *Icon*: A photograph,[17] icon, or sketch as a representation of the object, and in the case of concrete domains, an example of the object itself. It is such flexibility that makes sorting so readily usable in nonliterate contexts.

2. *Predication*: Objects are usually *names* of things (nouns, words, occupations, nations, vegetables ...), but there is no reason why this should be so. It is often more realistic to use *descriptions* of things ("the kind of x that ... "), or properties asserted about objects in a domain. In the occupations project it was found that people more naturally talk about

TABLE 1

Example of Three Sortings and Their Encoding

Domain	A set of eight vegetables: 1. beetroot, 2. cabbage, 3. carrot, 4. leek, 5. onion, 6. parsnip, 7. potato, 8. spinach, 9. sprout, 10. turnip
Method	Free-sorting

A: Data of 3 subjects (simple format) ("/" as separator between groups and "," as separator within groups)

R001 = {1, 3, 4, 5, 6, 7, 10 / 2, 8, 9}

    Groups   I: Root vegetables, II, Greens

R002 = {5, 7, 8, 10 / 2, 9 / 1, 3, 6 / 4}

    Groups   I: Boring, II: Overlapping leaves, III: Sweeter-tasting, IV: Doesn't fit

R003 = {2, 3, 4, 5, 6, 10 / 1, 7, 8, 9}

    Groups   I: Ones you'd use in a casserole, II: Ones you wouldn't

B: Dab in PDF:

Object: Subject:	1	2	3	4	5	6	7	8	9	10
R001	1	2	1	1	1	1	1	2	2	1
R002	3	2	3	4	1	3	1	1	2	1
R003	2	1	1	1	1	1	2	2	2	1

"the sort of people who ..." than about an occupation name itself, and predication—the assertion of some property to an object, the combination of a topic, and a comment on that topic (Miller, 1967, p. 26)—was a common component in images of occupations (Coxon and Jones, 1979c). A set of 50 descriptions of occupations was developed, and the descriptions were used as objects in their own right to define groups—clusters—of occupational characteristics, which were believed to go together.

3. *Instantiation*: A sorting of descriptions can be taken a stage further, so that when a subject has formed her categories of descriptions, she is handed the pack of object names and then asked to include (sort) the names into her descriptions category if she thought the object to be a typical instance of the group of descriptions or if she believed that the group of descriptions describe one or more objects. Obviously, this process of double-sorting can also be done in reverse, with the descriptions sorted into the categories of occupational names. However, using a set of objects as instances soon demonstrates two common problems with sorting methods. (1) Some instances may not describe any existing category (though that is a minor problem; these instances can simply feature as singletons). (2) More seriously, subjects may wish to sort the

same instance into more than one category, and in so doing break the main requirement that, in a partition, the groups must be mutually exclusive. Here by contrast, they will be overlapping.

4. *Overlapping categories*: At the theoretical level, overlapping categories pose no great problem; we have seen that prototypicality is often more important than ambiguity about borders, and mathematical developments such as "Fuzzy Sets" (Zadeh and Yager, 1987) have been created to address the issue of overlap directly. Rather than an element either belonging to or not belonging to a set in Fuzzy Set theory, there is a given *probability* that an element belongs to a given set. The main practical problem arises rather in statistical analysis of overlapping data, since almost all methods of analysis assume that sortings are partitions, and the set-theoretic properties that make arithmetic operations such as counting possible no longer hold when there is overlap. Consequently specially constructed measures are necessary for sorting data, which allow multiple assignment, such as the measures defined by Wing and Nelson (1972).

2.6.2. Variations Based on the Categories

Three common variants of sorting relate to the categories.

- *Fixed-sorting* is where the number (and sometimes the label) of the categories is fixed in advance for all subjects, and therefore features in the instructions ("... sort into *n* categories ...").

   In some instances, the number of categories is fixed, but no labels are attached to the categories. Fixed-category sorting is especially favored by Q methodology (see below), and Block (1956) argues that restricting the number of categories the subject is allowed to make has the advantage of standardizing the variance of the sorting categories. Borgatti (1992, p. 10) makes a similar point and recommends the practice on other grounds:

   > ... [using as many piles as the subject likes] ... is only helpful if respondents actually store relationships among items in mental piles. Since this is unlikely, there is little reason to feel guilty about imposing a restriction on the number of piles when necessary. Restricting the number of piles is necessary if you intend to compare individual informants' pile-sorts.

This advice is not necessarily well-founded and introduces the risk of distorting the subject's "natural" level of categorization (Rosch, 1977). Standardizing variation may be an attractive technical requirement, but it is rendered unnecessary by the existence of measures of co-occurrence, which build in information about category size (see Section 3.3.1) and comparison of individuals' sorting does not require equal number of categories if Arabie-Boorman measures are used. Indeed, Sherif and Sherif (1967) have argued that the number of categories a subject forms is directly related to a subject's involvement in the subject area, and equalizing categories will destroy this information.

But even when *free*-sorting is the main focus of data collection, researchers sometimes *restrict* the number of categories, either by excluding particular sortings (e.g., the "lumper," who puts all the objects into a single group, and the "splitter," who puts each object into a separate group) or by narrowing the range of the permitted number of groups (Bimler and Kirkland, 1998; Ben-Michael et al., 1997).

- *Graded-sorting* occurs where the categories (whether free or fixed) are required to be in rank-order. The most common example is the use of the Likert scale for categories, where the investigator prespecifies and labels the ordered categories (e.g., as in *Strongly Approve, Approve, Neither Approve nor Disapprove, Disapprove, Strongly Disapprove*). The ordering can also be done *after* the sorting, when the subject is instructed to put the categories he has formed into order on some specified criterion or is asked "whether there is an arrangement" in his categories (which invites but does not presuggest a rank-order).

- *Multiple sorts* occur when the subject makes more than one sorting of the same set of objects, either on the same criterion (as a test-retest reliability measure), or when the criterion is changed, as a test of innovativeness on the part of the subject. Multiple sorts can be used to change the context of categorization (e.g., occupational similarity and prestige can change dramatically when the criterion for sorting is changed from "social usefulness" to "prestige and reward they receive"). This variant is considered further below.

2.7. Three Special Cases of Sorting: Q Methodology, Multiple Sorts, and Hierarchies

Three variants of sorting have been developed to such an extent that they almost qualify as separate techniques, but they are so clearly special cases of sorting that they merit separate discussion.

2.7.1. Q Methodology

An important special case of fixed and graded sorting is Q methodology (Brown, 1986; McKeown and Thomas, 1988), which is a method developed initially in psychology to study subjectivity in a scientific manner. It has also been used extensively in the areas of political science (Brown, 1980) and health studies (Dennis, 1986; Larson, 1984). It differs from other sorting techniques in being much more restricted (both in the collection and in the analysis of the data) and in allying itself with an explicit methodological perspective of "scientific subjectivity of the person" (Stephenson, 1953).

Q methodology is termed "Q" to refer to the individual and his or her perspective as the locus of attention (as contrasted with conventional "R" analysis, where the interrelationship of variables is the main focus). The administration of the Q-sorting task is much the same as any other, but the respondent is constrained in the *number* of categories she may use, and the categories themselves are *ordered* at the outset, in a bipolar arrangement centering on a neutral category and having an equal number of categories on either side of the neutral category.[18] Moreover, the distribution is also sometimes predetermined by the researcher to follow a symmetric, bell-shaped quasinormal shape. This setup is illustrated in Figure 1.

In the administration of a Q-sort (McKeown and Thomas, 1988, pp. 31–33), the item cards are first divided into three groups: those the individual agrees with, those she is neutral/ambivalent/uncertain about, and those she disagrees with. Beginning at the *"most like my point of view"* extreme (or whatever other criterion is decided),

"Most *unlike* my point-of-view"					Neutral/ no salience			"Most *like* my point-of-view"			
−5	−4	−3	−2	−1	0	+1	+2	+3	+4	+5	(*weight*)
3	4	4	7	7	10	7	7	4	4	3	(*# of items*)
item	item	item	item	item	item	item	item	item	item	item	
item	item	item	item	item	item	item	item	item	item	item	
item	item	item	item	item	item	item	item	item	item	item	
	item	item	item	item	item	item	item	item	item		
			item	item	item	item	item				
			item	item	item	item	item				
			item	item	item	item	item				
					item						
					item						
					item						

Figure 1. Layout for 60-item, 11-point Q-Sort distribution.

she first chooses the n (fixed) items *closest* to her own point of view and locates them in the furthest left pile/category. She then shifts to the other extreme of the continuum and chooses the n (fixed) items *furthest* from her own point of view. After this, attention shifts from side to side, choosing the requisite number of items until the middle category is reached. As with the usual sorting, a subject is allowed to make adjustments and rearrangements at the end to secure closer representation of her point of view. Finally, Q-sorts are firmly, but by no means necessarily, wedded to the factor analytic model.

2.7.2. Multiple Sorting

The most detailed exposition and theoretical and methodological justification of multiple-sorting procedures has been by Canter and his colleagues (1985) and others in the Facet-theoretic tradition (Borg and Shye, 1995) and also by Rosenberg and Kim (1975). Canter et al. point out that sorting is a natural and more flexible special case of a number of other, more constrained, variants of data collection: pair comparisons, rankings, Q sorts, and semantic differential scales. As they use it, it differs from free sorting only in encouraging the respondent to "sort the elements, *using different criteria, a number of times*" (Canter et al., 1985, p. 88, emphasis added). Note that the respondent is usually free to define the criterion of sorting on each occasion, although in some variants a sequence of prescribed criteria is used. In the case of multiple sortings, the basic instructions for data collection thus need to be augmented, as in this example from Canter et al. (1985, pp. 88–89): "... when you have sorted the [objects] once I will ask you to *do it again*, using any different principles you can think of and we will carry on as many times as you feel able to produce different sorts ..." (emphasis in original).

Canter et al. report that the number of sortings normally carried out amount to "two or three, with seven and eight frequently possible, with 15 or more occurring in some cases" (1985, pp. 91–92). The range of the applications of multiple sortings to sociometric, architectural, environmental, and criminological contexts is extensive, and the use of Facet theory to define and guide analysis of the data is especially instructive (Borg and Shye, 1995; Gärling, 1976; Groat, 1982; Canter and King, 1996). Rosenberg and Kim (1975) have also argued for the use of multiple sorts as a matter of routine on the grounds that when subjects are told they may only make *one* sorting, they tend not to use the most "obvious" basis for their sorting, and this raises the possibility that normal single-sorting procedures may well bias the respondents to ignore more obvious or consensual bases for categorizations.

A particularly interesting and important variant of multiple sorting occurs when the initial exercise is repeated after some intervening experimental or intervention event. It thus becomes a form of pretest-intervention-posttest design. Trotter and Potter (1993) examined the feasibility of using sorting techniques for estimating the effects of an intervention program concerned with reducing risks associated with AIDS, alcohol consumption, and intravenous drugs use among a native American (Navaho) community. They first systematically sampled the range of risk areas by using a panel of both native Americans and cultural anthropologists and decided upon 41 types of risk in six areas: drug-related (e.g., sniffing something to get high), alcohol (drinking hard liquor), sexual/HIV-related (unprotected sex), school-related (dropping out of school), violence (beating someone up), together with traditional Navaho risk beliefs (walking around in a lightning storm). These 41 items were given to two groups of Navaho young men between 18 and 19 years of age for them to free-sort: a pretest group of 11 young men prior to their taking a Native American Community Association Awareness program concerning drugs, alcohol, and AIDS and a posttest group of 17 young men after the program; 6 took both the pretest and the posttest. The study went on to use multidimensional scaling and hierarchical clustering analysis on the data, and one significant fact was that although the same clusters of risk were evident in both pre- and posttest groups, the effect of the intervention was to "tighten up" the subjects' categorizations by making the constituent risks within a cluster much closer.

2.7.3. Hierarchy Construction

The hierarchy construction technique[19] is a more complex variant of free-sorting where the subject is asked to construct a hierarchy, consisting of a *set* of sortings of increasing generality. There are two main variants: the *agglomerative* (bottom-up) and the *divisive* (top-down) hierarchical sorting techniques.

- The agglomerative version begins with all the objects as separate groups (the splitter sorting) and proceeds to merge them until the single (lumper) sorting is obtained.

- The divisive version begins with the lumper sorting, then divides it down into two groups, which in turn are split into two at the next stage, until the splitter sorting is reached.

Agglomerative Hierarchical Sorting. The agglomerative hierarchy construction process begins with the subject being presented with all the objects, each of which is treated as a separate (singleton) group. He is then invited to join the two most similar objects as a *pair*. Having done so, he is then asked either to form another most similar pair or to add or *chain* one object to the existing pair. As this process continues, more than one cluster or category is usually formed, and a subject may then also merge or *join* two existing clusters. Finally, all the objects are clustered in one undifferentiated group. An example of a subject's hierarchy is reproduced in Figure 2.

In the example, he begins by putting the Actuary and the Chartered Accountant together as the most similar pair (level 1), then joins the Machine Tool Operator to the Carpenter as a pair (level 2). He then adds Solicitor to the existing Actuary-Chartered Accountant pair (level 3). His first merging of clusters is at level 10, where what he terms the "people-oriented" professions (Minister, Teacher) are

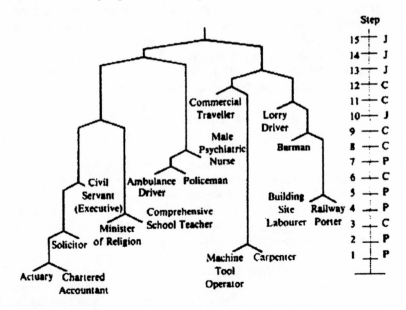

Figure 2. Example of an (agglomerative) hierarchy construction. (From Coxon and Davies, 1986, p. 146.)

joined to the "business/affairs" group to become "the professions." Having chained two more occupations to existing groups, he then merges two groups (level 13) to become "Working Class" and then merges a further two groups to become "Middle Class" (level 14).

Another way of thinking about an agglomerative hierarchy is as a nested set of levels, *each* of which constitutes a sorting, from the initial level where each object is a separate group, to the final sorting, where there is a single undifferentiated group. Starting at the bottom, each higher level is a "coarser" (less fine) sorting or partition than the one below it. The method of free-sorting can thus be thought of as an "arrested" hierarchy construction. The point at which a subject stops a sorting can be construed as being her "basic-level" of categorization—"the most inclusive (abstract) level at which the categories can mirror the structure of attributes perceived in the world" (Rosch, 1978, pp. 30–31; Rosch et al., 1976).

Divisive Hierarchical Sorting. This divisive variant of hierarchical sorting was first described explicitly by Boster (1986) and is akin to the taxonomy-construction task described above as an eliciting procedure. The difference is that divisive hierarchical sorting is a *binary* splitting technique, since at each stage a group is split into two (and no more) subgroups. The subject is presented with a deck of cards and asked to divide it into two groups, which will usually be of different sizes. Each group in turn is further divided into two piles, and this process continues until the subject either decides that a pile should not be split any further or finishes with all objects in a separate piles.

There exist a number of instances of hybrid mixtures of free-sorting and hierarchies:

- *sorting followed by (upward) merging,*[20] where the subject first makes a free-sorting and is then asked to continue to merge the categories, as in the hierarchies method, until a single group is made.
- *sorting followed by (downward) division* (Clark, 1968), where after making an initial sorting, the subject is then asked to divide down the (nonsingleton) groups into further groups of greater internal homogeneity.
- *sorting followed by both downward division and upward merging,* the G/P/A (grouping, partitioning, adding) technique recently developed by Kirkland et al. (1998). The subject first performs a free-sorting, to produce the initial groups (grouping). If any of his groups have more than three objects, he is then invited to divide it down further into more

homogeneous groups (partitioning). Then he is asked to merge (adding) the existing groups, progressively relaxing the similarity criteria until a very few "supergroups" remain. In effect this identifies three stages in the construction of a hierarchy: a low stage (grouping followed by partition), a moderate stage (the initial grouping), and a high stage (grouping followed by addition).

Although the method of hierarchical sorting gives much more detailed data than free-sorting, the detail is bought at the cost of reducing numbers drastically; it is rarely feasible with more than 25 objects because of the complexity of the task and the consequent cognitive strain involved.

Finally, the rating or ranking of the objects (or, indeed, the subject's groupings) is a common method used in combination with sorting, and this leads to a composite methodology called "perceptual mapping" (Bimler and Kirkland, 1998) and "concept mapping" (Trochim, 1989). The former approach develops a novel "hot-spot" model that integrates information from a subject's (or a group's) sorting into a (multidimensional scaling) perceptual map as points of high salience (Kirkland et al., 1998). The latter approach, implemented as a Windows package called CONCEPT-SYSTEMS (see Appendix 4 on website) uses procedures similar to those described in this book and consists of a number of linked procedures:

- *eliciting a domain*, usually using focus group or brainstorming procedures to generate several large numbers of statements from participants.
- *systematic data collection*, using free-sorting techniques, followed by rating of the descriptions.
- *data analysis*, using multidimensional scaling and hierarchical clustering techniques.

In these composite variants of sorting, external information such as ratings or rankings (or even separate sortings) of the same objects can be embedded in the space obtained by multidimensional scaling (see Section 4.2.1) to interpret it better or to combine sorting analysis with rankings and ratings of the same objects.

2.8. An Example

The Coastal North Carolina Socioeconomic Study (Maiolo et al., 1993) is one of the most extensive examples of the use of sorting methodology and related methods. With the possibility of gas and oil exploration along the Outer Continental Shelf of the area, a study was set up to explore the socioeconomic and sociocultural conditions of the area prior to any such development. Eight coastal communities were chosen, and respondents were recruited from among the inhabitants. As a preliminary step to the sorting studies, free-listing was used to elicit contents of three relevant domains: *Qualities of the Area, Uses of the Environment*, and *Perceptions of Change*, and 24, 20, and 24 commonly occurring items, respectively, were used as objects for further analysis. For example, the items included:

Qualities of the Area:
> People share a sense of community
> The beaches are clean

Uses of the Environment:
> Off-shore recreational fishing
> Windsurfing

Perceptions of Change:
> Sewage problems
> Unplanned developments

These objects were then used in a number of pile-sorting exercises, both with the original respondents and also with 20 respondents from local government, business, and other groups in the communities. The free-sorting format used a general criterion of similarity, and respondents were asked to name their groups. Next, they were given a set of items representing desirable attributes for communities and asked to sort them into a five-point (Likert) ordered scale in terms of how accurately the statements described their community.

The attraction of this particular study from the point of view of the methodologist and researcher is that details of the individual listings, sorting, and names of groups are published in full, making it possible to replicate the study findings and use other techniques. Equally, it is easy to see how the findings relate to a highly policy-relevant set of issues. The analysis of these data were performed with a commonly used range of methods explained in later chapters (multidimensional scaling, hierarchical clustering, property-fitting, and cultural consensus measurement) and were implemented using the ANTHROPAC package.

3. DESCRIBING AND COMPARING SORTINGS

It is perhaps a consequence of the deceptive simplicity of the method of sorting that so many of its problematic aspects have remained unexamined.
Boorman and Arabie (1972, p. 248)

In this chapter we examine and evaluate methods used (1) to describe the characteristics and structural properties of single sortings (partitions), (2) to compare (and measure the proximity of) several sortings on a pairwise basis (i.e., between subjects), and (3) to describe structural properties of the objects, based on the aggregated sortings.

3.1. Properties of Single Sortings

Three variables describe the sorting that each subject makes. Two relate to structure, (1) the number of categories she forms and (2) the relative size of her groups, and one to content, namely, (3) the actual composition of her categories.

There are two extreme types of sorting: at one extreme is the *splitter* (each object forms its own group, so there are as many groups as there are objects), and at the other extreme the *lumper* (where all objects are in the same, single, group). Together these define the ends of a continuum referred to as the "lumper-splitter axis." Cognitively these extreme cases can be thought of in terms of a subject who recognizes no *similarity* or communality between the objects in the set (the splitter) and one who recognizes no *differences* between them and therefore does not discriminate among them (the lumper). All other possible sortings lie between these extremes.

The actual number of groups used by a subject should not by itself be given too much weight, although Sherif and Hovland (1953) and others have argued that, at least when sorting attitude items, the actual number of categories used by a subject is *inversely* related to her degree of involvement. More important is the combined information on the number *and* size of the groups. In many instances, the sorting made by a subject will contain several singleton groups (consisting of one object), which in effect do not fit into her categorization.

3.1.1. The Height Measure

The main concern is therefore to describe what is variously referred to as the "height" or "shape" or "lumpiness" (Johnson, 1967; Boorman and Arabie, 1972; Arabie and Boorman, 1973) of a sorting. The "height" of a partition [referred to here as h(P) and identical to Arabie's D(P); see Appendix 1 on website] consists simply of the sum over all groups of the number of pairs in each of the groups:

$$\text{(raw) height: } h(k) = \sum_i \binom{c_i}{2} = \sum c_i(c_i - 1)/2$$

That is, the height of subject k's sorting consists of counting the pairs within each of his categories (c_i) and adding them together. For example, taking R002's sorting in Table 1 (see Chapter 2), R002 has four groups, the first has 4 elements, (hence 6 pairs); the second has 2 elements (1 pair); the third has 3 elements (3 pairs), and the fourth has 1 element and hence 0 pairs, so $h(\text{R002}) = 10$. By contrast, R003 has 2 groups, and his height measure is 21, and R001 also has two groups, and a higher height value $h(\text{R001}) = 24$. Thus, we would say that R003 is considerably more "lumpy" (has larger height value) than R002, and R001 is yet more "lumpy."

It can easily be seen that the more compact a sorting is (in the sense that it comprises groups with a large number of elements) the more pairs (or "pairbonds") there are and the greater the "height." The height measure is therefore a measure of co-occurrence of pairs within a group or of the aggregativeness of a subject's sortings.

The height measure has other intuitively acceptable properties. Consider a domain set of p elements. The "lumper" has a maximum "height" of $p(p - 1)/2$ whereas the splitter has a minimum height of 0, and these two cases define the two ends of a the lumper-splitter axis. The height measure for all possible sortings of six elements is illustrated in Figure 3.[21]

The following points are worth commenting on.

1. Several distinct sortings have the same height value. Hence "height" does not uniquely identify a sorting, only some properties of it.
2. By using pairs as the basic unit, large subgroups contribute substantially to the height measure, hence strongly indicating tendencies toward "lumping."

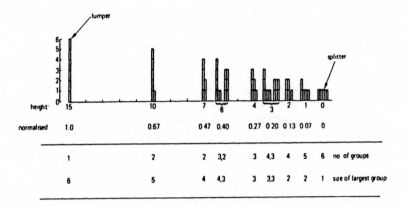

Figure 3. Height measure and properties of six-element partitions. (From Coxon and Jones, 1979a, p. 22.)

3. However, both the number of groups and the size of the largest group in a sorting are ordinally (weakly monotonically) related to height—the former in a decreasing manner, and the latter in an increasing manner.

This simple height measure thus provides a useful characterization of the "shape" of a sorting or of the *way* in which subjects demarcate the set of objects. Typically, the researcher will wish to know, for instance, what the distribution of height measures is, and whether it relates in any systematic way to independent variables such as gender, age, life history, and so forth.

As it stands, the (raw) height measure depends on the number of objects in the domain set. Often it is necessary to compare height values across domains of different size, and for this purpose it is convenient to define a normalized height value, defined between 0 (the splitter) and 1 (the lumper). This is done by dividing raw height value by its maximum value, that of the lumper:

$$\text{Normalized height: } = \frac{\Sigma_i (c_i)(c_i - 1)/2}{p(p - 1)/2}$$

where p is the number of objects in the domain.

Returning to the example; there are 45 pairs in a 10-object set—the height of the lumper—so R002's normalized height value is 0.22 (10/45), R003's is 0.47 (21/45), and R001's is 0.53.

3.2. Comparing Individuals' Sortings (Pairwise)

How may the sortings of two subjects be compared? To what extent are categorizations shared? To answer these questions, it is necessary (1) to compare the composition of the subjects' groupings and (2) to define some form of similarity measure between them.

If two people produce two identical sortings they presumably do so with respect to the same features, that is, the groups probably mean the same to each person. It would be useful to denote such a case by total similarity or zero distance. Total *dis*similarity is fairly easy to define in terms of the lumper and the splitter—for who could be more dissimilar (distant) with respect to their sortings than those who make every object unique and those who make no differentiation between the objects?

3.2.1. The Intersection Matrix

Since the order of the groups in a sorting is arbitrary, comparison can best be done by looking at the *overlap* between two individual's sortings. This is done by defining an *intersection matrix* (denoted **Z**) between the two partitions, akin to the cross-tabulation table except that the rows of the intersection table refer to each group/category of subject X and the columns refer to each of subject Y's groups/categories, and the entries in the table itself consist of the objects themselves. This table plays a crucial role in the development of measures of similarity in sorting. The intersection matrix between R001 and R003 provides a useful illustration (Figure 4).

The rows in Figure 4B are labeled with R001's two categories and the columns with R003's two categories. Each entry $z(i, j)$ in the table consists of the intersection of (the objects common to) both category i of R001 *and* category j of R003. For instance, in $z(1, 1)$ there are 5 vegetables that are in R001's category$_1$ (Root vegetables) and also in R003's category$_1$ (Casserole) and in $z(2, 1)$ there is the only vegetable common to R001's Greens and R003's Casserole, namely "2. cabbage."

A: Subjects' sortings:
Objects: {1. *beetroot*, 2. *cabbage*, 3. *carrot*, 4. *leek*, 5. *onion*, 6. *parsnip*,
  7. *potato*, 8. *spinach*, 9. *sprout*, 10. *turnip*}
R001   {1,3,4,5,6,7,10 / 2,8,9}
  I: Root vegetables, II: Greens
R002   {5,7,8,10 / 2,9 / 1,3,6 / 4}
  I: Boring, II: Overlapping leaves, III: Sweeter-tasing, IV: Doesn't fit
R003   {2,3,4,5,6,10 / 1,7,8,9}
  I: Ones you'd use in a casserole; II: Ones you wouldn't

B: Intersection table (**Z**): R001 & R003

R001: \ R003:	*Casserole*	*Not Casserole*
Root vegetables	3. carrot, 4. leek, 5. onion, 6. parsnip, 10. turnip	1. beetroot, 7. potato
Greens	2. cabbage	8. spinach, 9. sprout

C: PAIRBONDS measure of dissimilarity between R001's and R003's sortings

h(R001)	$= 21 + 3$	$= 24$
h(R003)	$= 15 + 6$	$= 21$
h(R001 & R003)	$= 10 + 1 + 0 + 1$	$= 12$
PAIRBONDS (X, Y)	$= h(X) + h(Y) - 2 \times h(X \& Y)$	
PAIRBONDS (R001, R003)	$= 24 + 21 - 2 \times 12$	$= 21$

Figure 4. Intersection of two sortings and PAIRBONDS measure.

The significance of the (nonempty) entries in the intersection table is that, taken together, they can be considered as forming a sorting or partition *in its own right*. This partition is "finer"[22] than the partition of either subject and is the one from which both their sortings can be built up by a process of logical addition (the union of subsets).

In the case of two identical sortings, the **Z** matrix will contain exactly the same groups that each of the subjects has. Where, by contrast, the lumper meets the splitter, the matrix will turn into one long row (or column) with one object in each cell. Moreover, from a reading of the **Z** matrix it is possible to detect whether two subjects' groups are the same (equivalent in composition), or one subject's group is a subset of the other's group:

- A category c_i of subject X and a category d_j of subject Y are *equivalent* if $z(i, j)$ is not empty, but all other entries in the row i *and* all other entries in the column j of **Z** are empty.
- A category c_i of subject X is a (*proper*) *subset*[23] of the category d_j of subject Y if $z(i, j)$ is not empty, but all other entries in the row i are empty.
- A category d_j of subject Y is a (*proper*) *subset* of the category c_i of subject X if $z(j, i)$ is not empty, but all other entries in the column j are empty.

These conditions are illustrated in Figure 5.

In this schematic intersection table, an X signifies that there must be one or more objects in that cell, 0 means that the cell concerned must have no entries, and the empty cells in the table may or may not have entries.

The relevance of finding subsets and equivalence of this sort is that it makes it possible not only to recognize categories with identical contents, but also to detect differing degrees of fineness or generality in what amounts to the same category system, for if X's sorting differs from Y's sorting only in further dividing X's categories, the two category systems differ only in that Y's is a finer partition (less general) than X's. Moreover, if the tendency to split is only an aspect of individual style or reflects simply a high degree of interest in the domain, then the fact that Y subdivides a category that she otherwise shares with X is of less significance than the fact that they share a common category.

Another use of detecting equivalence is that it allows differences in types of category meaning to be recognized, since it allows identity of reference (equivalence in composition of categories) and identity of sense (equivalence in names assigned to categories) to be distinguished.

If the categories have been labeled or described by the subjects, then the researcher can do two things:

- *equivalence of sense*: Identify any categories that have been given the same name. Intersect the sortings of those involved, two at a time,[24]

		Subject 1:		
		I	II	III
Subject 2:	A			0
	B	0	0	X
	C			0

1: Subject 2's category B *equals* subject 1's category III
$z(B, III) > 0$ *and other cells in row B and in column III are* 0   (B = III)

		Subject 1:		
		I	II	III
Subject 2:	A	X	0	0
	B			
	C			

2: Subject 2's category A *is a (proper) subset of* subject 1's category I
$z(A, I) > 0$ *and other cells in row A are* 0   (A ⊂⊂ I)

		Subject 1:		
		I	II	III
Subject 2:	A		0	
	B		0	
	C		X	

3: Subject 1's category II *is a (proper) subset of* subject 2's category C
$z(C, II) > 0$ *and other cells in column II are* 0   (II ⊂⊂ C)

Figure 5. Equivalence and subsets in two subjects' sortings.

and examine the overlap. This can be a way of investigating communality and consensus and also prototypicality in a category system.

- *equivalence of reference*: Identify categories from different subjects that are identical in composition and examine the names and descriptions given to them to see what (similar and different) meaning and labels are being invoked.

36

3.2.2. Pairwise Proximity Measures Between Subjects' Sortings

A most striking development of recent years has been a renewed interest in "least-move" measures for assessing association and similarity, more recently extended to cover sortings as partitions (Boorman and Arabie, 1972; Barthélemy et al., 1984; see also Day (1986). Following Kendall's (1962) idea of counting the number of order-inversions between two sets of ranks to measure ordinal correlation,[25] and Kemeny and Snell's (1972) idea of examining the number of changes necessary to turn one rank ordering into another, an analogous family of measures is also available for assessing the similarity between (and consensus among) free-sortings, based on measures that have been developed to compare partitions of a set. Arabie and Boorman (Boorman and Arabie, 1972; Arabie and Boorman, 1973) have given the main accessible expositions of the area and have systematized and integrated a family of distance measures for partitions (and therefore individual sortings). Their treatment is followed in this section (Figure 6 and Appendix 1 on website), and their notation and names of the measures are followed throughout the text. Arabie and Hubert (1992) provide an overview and bibliography of this entire area.

The central characteristic of measures between sortings is based upon the simple idea of seeing how many moves or reallocations are necessary to change one sorting into another[26] [see also Mirkin (1975) for a related approach]. A distance measure between two sortings X and Y is then defined as the minimum number of simple moves necessary to transform sorting X into sorting Y. In the case of similar or proximate sortings, few moves will be necessary, but for dissimilar or distant ones a large number of moves will be needed. There is, however, one important proviso: there are different ways of defining such a simple or elemental move, each of which defines a different family of measures.

Transformations of particular interest to the empirical researcher (in part simply because of the simplicity of their interpretation) are the PAIRBONDS move (D) and subset-move (APPROX) transformations (and their normalizations when relevant).

3.2.2.1. Pairbonds Dissimilarity Measure.
The PAIRBONDS measure is a simple extension of the height measure discussed above. Of

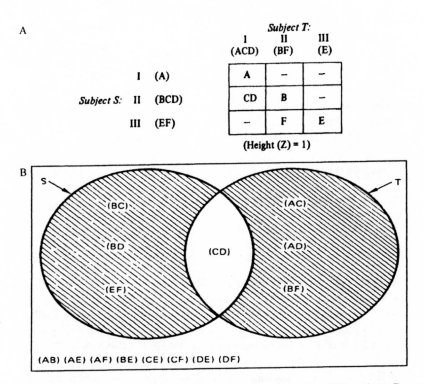

Figure 6. The PAIRBONDS measure. A. Intersection of S and T sortings. B. PAIRBONDS and symmetric difference of pairs. (From Coxon and Jones, 1979a, p. 28.)

all the metrics, D (PAIRBONDS) is the most readily interpreted and most frequently used (under a variety of names and versions). It has been defined for sociometric and graph-theoretic data (as the symmetric difference of pairs) by Restle (1959) and Flament (1962), for comparing partitions/sortings and dendograms by Frank (1975, 1976), for co-occurrence data by Rapoport and Fillenbaum (1972), for clustering solutions by Rand (1971), and for partition distance in general by Mirkin and Chernyi (1970) and Hubert and Arabie (1985).

$$\text{PAIRBONDS} = D(P, Q)$$

$$= D(P) + D(Q) - 2(P \& Q)$$

where D is the height measure.

The easiest way of interpreting PAIRBONDS is as being the symmetric difference of the pairbonds in P's and Q's sorting. Consider the following example illustrated in Figure 6A.

S's sorting consists of: {A / B, C, D / E, F}   with a height (D) value of 4

T's sorting consists of: {A, C, D / B, F / E}   with a height value of 4.

The intersection matrix S & T   has a height value of 1.
The PAIRBONDS value is therefore: $4 + 4 - (2 \times 1) = 6$.

Figure 6B shows the result as a Venn diagram of the 15 possible pairs; 8 pairs are in neither sorting, and 1 pair (C, D) is in both. The shaded area makes up the "symmetric difference" of the sorting pairs: 3 pairs are in S's but not T's sorting and 3 pairs are in T's but not in S's sorting—these constitute the PAIRBONDS value. Flament (1962, pp. 15–17) proves that the symmetric difference, and therefore PAIRBONDS, is a metric, satisfying non-negativity, symmetry, and the triangle inequality (see Appendix 2 on website). It is a "minimum-move" measure relating to pairs, for its value gives the number of pairs that need to be reallocated to turn one partition into the other.

PAIRBONDS can be normalized between 0 and 1. The simplest way is to take the total number of pairs as denominator. Arabie and Boorman (1973) propose two other forms, a "strong" normalization (with two variants based on the sum and the geometric mean of the height values of the two sortings) and a "mild" normalization. The effects of these apparently innocuous normalizations on the scaling representation is mentioned below.

3.2.2.2. Rand Index. In a similar manner, Rand (1971) and Hubert and Arabie (1985) examine the similarity between any two sortings S and T by considering how each pair of objects is assigned in each sorting. They do this by first defining the four possible types of agreement and disagreement that can exist between how a pair of objects is allocated in the two sortings:

Type	Description
	Objects in the pair:
I	Put in same category in both S and in T.
II	Put in different categories in S and also in different categories in T.
III	Put in different categories in S and in same category in T.
IV	Put in same category in S and in different categories in T.

These four types correspond to the four regions of Figure 6B, and their counts can be derived directly from the intersection table (details and equations are contained in Appendix 3 on website).

The number of pairs in types I and II comprise the *agreements* (A) and the number of pairs in types III and IV comprise the *disagreements* (D) between the two partitions. Intuitively, partitions that are similar produce high A values and low values of D. There have been several measures of partition proximity based on the A and D values, including most notably:

- Rand (1971) who uses:

$$A \bigg/ \binom{p}{2}$$

  to define the similarity measure termed the Rand Index.
- Johnson (1967), Mirkin and Chernyi (1970), and Arabie and Boorman (1973) who all use

$$D \bigg/ \binom{p}{2}$$

  as their basic dissimilarity measure.
- Hubert (1977), who uses the difference to define his measure:

$$(A - D) \bigg/ \binom{p}{2}$$

The Rand Index[27] has been used extensively to measure the distance between dendograms (clustering trees) as well as partitions, and Hubert and Arabie (1985) discuss its properties and also ways of correcting the measure for chance and normalizing it.[28]

3.2.2.3. "APPROX": Dissimilarity Measure. The minimum set-move measure (called "APPROX" by Arabie and Boorman) is defined as:

$$APPROX = |P \& Q| - \min(|P|, |Q|)$$

where $|A|$ denotess the number of (nonzero) cells or categories in a partition A.

It also has an attractive interpretation: it is the number of *set-moves* necessary to transform one sorting into the other (Boorman and Arabie, 1972, pp. 230–231). Its disadvantage is that it yields few distinct values which can be a problem for ordinal scaling. To see what the set-moves amount to, consider the following example drawn from Boorman and Arabie: using the set $\{1, 2, 3, 4, 5, 6, 7, 8\}$

$$P = \{1 / 2,3,4,7,8 / 5,6\} \quad (|P| = 3) \quad \text{and}$$

$$Q = \{1,2 / 3,4 / 5,6 / 7,8\} \quad (|Q| = 4)$$

Intersection matrix P & Q =

P: \ Q:	d_1	d_2	d_3	d_4
c_1	1			
c_2	2	3, 4		7, 8
c_3		5, 6		

so $|P \& Q| = 5$. Hence

$$APPROX = 5 - \min(3, 4) = 2.$$

The two permissible set-moves are:

• (type I) to transfer a subset into a different cell/category, and
• (type II) to transfer a subset to form a new cell/category.

The two-step sequence necessary to turn P into Q are as follows:

Start: $P = \{1 \ / \ 2, 3, 4, 7, 8 \ / \ 5, 6\}$

    Step 1: Form a new cell by transferring the subset $\{7, 8\}$ out of the second category into a new category (type II set-move), making $\{1 \ /2, 3, 4 \ / \ 5, 6 \ / \ 7, 8\}$.

    Step 2: Transfer the subset $\{2\}$ out of the second category into the first category (type I set-move), making $\{1, 2 \ / \ 3, 4 \ / \ 5, 6 \ / \ 7, 8\}$, which is the sorting Q.

End.

These are the two moves that make up the APPROX value.

The remaining measures in the Arabie-Boorman set are mostly information-theoretic measures (Donderi, 1988). The information-theoretic measures are also minimum-move measures (now of the *amount of information* necessary to turn one sorting into another). However, they have rarely been used to analyze sortings, consequently, their properties are not well understood and they are not discussed further.

Finally, it is worth remembering that the intersection matrix between two individual sortings is as much a cross-tabulation as the more usual contingency table or cross-classification of two *variables*. In this more familiar form, the categories of the two variables form the rows and columns of the table, and the entries in the table consist of the number of respondents who have the same combination of categories. In the present case, however, it is the two *individuals* sorting categories that are the "variables," and the entries in the table are a count of the number of *elements* that share the same combination of categories. Consequently, it is not surprising that there is also a set of measures based upon traditional nominal scale measures of contingency and association (CHISQUAR and 1-LAMBDA in Appendix 1 on website), and in principle many more could be added.

3.3. Comparing Objects (Co-Occurrence)

In the normal way, the main concern of the researcher is to examine the relationships between the objects in the sorting (so-called

R analysis) and obtain a measure of proximity between them. This is almost always done by looking at the extent to which objects occur together in the same group in the subjects' sortings. Co-occurrence consequently plays a central role in measuring the similarity between objects.

Although the preferred data format for a subject's sorting (see Section 2.5 above) is the row vector containing the group number to which each object was sorted, this is not the most convenient form of data representation for aggregating sortings. The sorting of p objects by any individual i can be represented as a square co-occurrence matrix C^i of order p. The entries in this matrix, C^i_{jk}, contain 1 if objects j and k both occur in the same category of her sorting and is 0 otherwise. This is variously referred to as a co-occurrence, an adjacency, or an incidence matrix.

Thus, the individual's sorting $P = \{3, 1 \ / \ 4, 2, 5\}$ can be represented by the $(0, 1)$ co-occurrence matrix:

$$
\begin{bmatrix}
- & 0 & 1 & 0 & 0 \\
0 & - & 0 & 1 & 1 \\
1 & 0 & - & 0 & 0 \\
0 & 1 & 0 & - & 1 \\
0 & 1 & 0 & 1 & -
\end{bmatrix}
$$

($n.b.$ Diagonal elements are ignored.)

The most intuitively obvious measure of the similarity between the objects (derived from the set of subjects' sortings) is simply to add these individual co-occurrence matrices, C^i to form a single aggregate co-occurrence or "abundance" matrix C, whose entries c_{jk} represent the frequency with which object j and object k are put into the same group—in this case, the number of subjects who put both j and k in the same group in their respective sortings. So that if all of the subjects put the two objects together, there is maximum similarity, and if none of them do, there is minimum similarity.

The properties of this simple aggregated co-occurrence measure (referred to sometimes as the F measure, and here simply as M1) have been discussed by Miller (1967, pp. 191–194), and it is used extensively as a basis for analyzing sorting data. The co-occurrence values provide a useful gradation of similarity compared with the dichotomous "belonging/not belonging" characteristic of a single sorting. The highest co-occurrence values signal overwhelming consensus on what goes with what (on whatever basis the allocation has been made), and the objects involved may well be prototypical examples. Similarly, the lowest values signal dissociation, and a zero value means that no subjects, whatever the bases of their sorting, put them together (whether this is because they share no characteristic in common is a moot point). In between, there are a whole set of relative similarities, and these make it possible for an analysis procedure to work.

An example of such an aggregate co-occurrence matrix is given in Figure 7 (in lower-triangle form, since co-occurrences are obviously symmetric). The table reports how many (of 71 subjects) put the row occupation and the column occupation into the same category of their sortings (Coxon and Jones, 1979a, p. 42; Coxon and Jones, 1979b, p. 170). In fact, there is no pair of occupations that everyone puts in the same category (the closest is Plumber and Carpenter, two classic—and prototypical—"Trades" occupations, that 90% of the subjects put together). At the other extreme there are a few pairs that no one puts together, and these are at opposite extremes in terms of of the prestige: Barman with Geologist and with Eye Surgeon.

Sometimes a similarity (or "proximity") measure is inconvenient,[29] and it is better to operate with a dissimilarity measure. This is easily done by reversing the co-occurrence measure into a dissimilarity measure δ by the following equation:

$$\delta_{i,j} = (\text{max} - c_{i,j})$$

where max is the total number of subjects, and hence the highest possible co-occurrence value. As such, it satisfies the requirements of a metric (see Appendix 2 on website). It has been commented on that the measure is also well-behaved in the scaling sense, and it is very widely used (see, for example, Anglin, 1970; Fillenbaum and Rapoport, 1971; Burton, 1972; Coxon and Jones, 1979a; Rosenberg, 1982) and is the normal default in most sorting packages.

	CA	SST	GM	BM	ST	SW	C	AD	CPR	MOR	PL	MPN	BCK	PST	UMO	PM	CE	PHT	BSL	RCK	AP	A	RED	PO	GEO	SMG	TDH	TDR	ESG	JN	LT
SST	25																														
GM	3	2																													
BM	3	2	9																												
ST	43	29	2	2																											
SW	13	40	6	3	17																										
C	2	1	61	11	2	5																									
AD	2	4	21	21	3	12	19																								
CPR	27	17	8	5	2	19	6	4																							
MOR	26	43	3	10	32	39	3	7	12																						
PL	4	2	58	5	20	26	64	17	7	4																					
MPN	10	22	13	8	3	6	12	20	19	25	13																				
BCK	22	16	10	10	9	39	9	11	33	11	10	22																			
PST	15	54	3	5	23	47	2	8	21	3	3	28	27																		
UMO	1	1	17	2	20	3	16	22	3	15	15	8	7	2																	
PM	6	16	10	39	2	29	7	25	17	17	8	27	29	21	7																
CE	45	27	8	12	34	14	17	1	26	6	9	12	8	16	3	14															
PHT	5	1	1	1	7	8	7	8	15	1	18	16	5	6	5	6	7														
BSL	1	15	16	11	8	1	17	20	2		19	6	16	8	63	18	3	5													
RCK	4	1	36	42	2	9	20	20	13		35	16	9	9	18	4	31	20	20												
AP	26	4	10	28	15	11	37	3	22	17	7	9	5	8	4	11	10	35	3	7											
A	10	8	7	10	12	12	8	32	14	15	33	7	16	9	3	9	5	18	11	11	10										
RED	5	3	35	7	3	6	7	3	4	3	7	8	3	3	1	20	5	3	6	12	6	7									
PO	2	2	13	5	37	13	12	35	3	26	8	12	7	16	34	25	46	1	8	22	25	3	18								
GEO	37	37	0	3	1	26	24	25	24	15	3	11	12	19	1	7	14	3	14	3	11	13	8	1							
SMG	25	25	7	7	7	25	3	25	25	1	19	9	11	8	2	8	2	8	14	6	18	20	6	6	14						
TDH	2	2	16	38	3	2	18	4	4	14	3	7	26	13	1	8	11	13	8	10	8	3	17	34	3	2					
TDR	2	2	18	35	19	5	14	15	13	1	19	9	7	3	2	15	3	3	6	19	13	8	32	36	3	10	25				
ESG	33	3	3	0	21	20	8	4	17	35	21	25	5	22	8	20	37	37	14	6	30	10	5	2	34	24	2	1			
JN	11	17	9	3	19	19	2	4	17	19	21	12	16	19	3	20	14	14	19	18	15	39	12	4	18	18	4	8	10		
LT	12	8	23	7	10	16	23	15	35	10	21	27	21	11	8	20	14	14	6	19	20	18	18	51	11	18	6	3	13	3	
BC	2	2	14	39	3	3	12	33	2	2	12	9	9	3	37	15	6	38	18	18	9	4	23	51	2	5	38	44	1	3	5

(BC)

45

Occupational Title*	Abbreviation	Occupational Title*	Abbreviation
1 Chartered Accountant	CA	17 Civil Engineer	CE
2 Secondary School Teacher	SST	18 Photographer	PHT
3 Garage Mechanic	GM	19 Building Site Labourer	BSL
4 Barman	BM	20 Restaurant Cook	RCK
5 Statistician	ST	21 Airline Pilot	AP
6 Social Worker	SW	22 Actor	A
7 Carpenter	C	23 Railway Engine Driver	RED
8 Ambulance Driver	AD	24 Postman	PO
9 Computer Programmer	CPR	25 Geologist	GEO
10 Minister of Religion	MOR	26 Sales Manager	SMG
11 Plumber	PL	27 Trawler Deckhand	TDH
12 Male Psychiatric Nurse	MPN	28 Taxi Driver	TDR
13 Bank Clerk	BCK	29 Eye Surgeon	ESG
14 Primary School Teacher	PST	30 Journalist	JN
15 Unskilled Machine Operator in a factory assembly line	UMO	31 Laboratory Technician	LT
16 Policeman	PM	32 Bus Conductor	BCR

Figure 7. Co-occurrence matrix from 71 sortings of occupational titles. Entries in the matrix are the number of individuals (out of 71) who put the row occupation and the column occupation into the same category. (From Coxon and Jones, 1979b, p. 170.)

46

3.3.1. Taking Account of Differential Category Size: Burton's Measures

The main deficiencies of the simple co-occurrence measure are two-fold.

- It does not allow for individual differences in sorting. In particular, it does not take into account the *size* of the category from which co-occurrences come—so that the fact that a pair (j, k) occurs in the sorting of a subject has the same weight in determining similarity, whether it comes from a large or a small category.
- It does not take into account information about pairs that are *not* put together.

It may make sense, therefore, to take such factors into account before aggregating into overall similarity.[30] Burton (1975) proposes a series of four proximity measures all based upon co-occurrence frequencies, but which *do* take these factors into account. He modifies Miller's original similarity measure slightly to satisfy the technical axiom of positivity of a metric, and when thus corrected he goes on to define his family of co-occurrence measures. They all have the same form, but differ in how the individual (unaggregated) similarity counts are (re-)defined.

For all four measures, each individual's contribution to overall similarity is a weighted function of his $(0, 1)$ co-occurrence measure and the different forms of the weighting factor represent differing assumptions about the individual's sorting.

Burton's weighted similarity measures are defined:

$$S_{j,k}^{(i)} = a\left(C_{j,k}^{(i)}\right),$$

where $C_{j,k}^{(i)}$ is the $(0, 1)$ occurrence of j and k in subject i's sorting and a is the weighting factor.

Measure 1 (M1): Unit Weighting (Miller's Co-Occurrence; Burton's F). This is the basic measure. In this case, attention is simply paid to whether or not $(1, 0)$ a pair of objects occur in the same category—no matter what the size of the category—and therefore no attention is paid to any differential discrimination the subject may make. Since each co-occurrence contributes equally, the aggregate matrix **C** is the simple sum of the individual matrices. In the case of the example specified above, the individual's sorting $(P = \{3, 1 / 4, 2, 5\})$ is thus:

$$
\begin{bmatrix}
— & 0 & 1 & 0 & 0 \\
0 & — & 0 & 1 & 1 \\
1 & 0 & — & 0 & 0 \\
0 & 1 & 0 & — & 1 \\
0 & 1 & 0 & 1 & —
\end{bmatrix}
$$

Measure 2 (M2): Weighting by Category Size (Burton's F'). The entry in the individual co-occurrence matrix is the number of objects in the category from which the pair is drawn. Hence, the larger the category in which a pair of objects occur, the higher their similarity is considered to be. Because big cells make larger contributions to similarity than small cells, it implies that objects which occur in the large groups are more similar than those which appear in small groups. The effect will be to emphasize gross discriminations on the part of the subject, and the tendency toward "lumpiness." In the example, the individual co-occurrence matrix with M2 would be:

$$
\begin{bmatrix}
— & 0 & 2 & 0 & 0 \\
0 & — & 0 & 3 & 3 \\
2 & 0 & — & 0 & 0 \\
0 & 3 & 0 & — & 3 \\
0 & 3 & 0 & 3 & —
\end{bmatrix}
$$

Measure 3 (M3): Weight by Reciprocal of Category Size (Burton's G). The entry in the individual co-occurrence matrix is now the *reciprocal* of the number of objects in the category from which the pair is drawn. Hence, the smaller the category in which a pair of objects occur, the higher their similarity is considered to be. Because small cells make larger contributions to similarity than large cells, it implies that objects which occur in the smaller groups are more similar than those which appear in larger groups. The effect will be to emphasize fine discriminations on the part of the subject, and the tendency toward "splitting." In the example, the individual co-occurrence matrix would be:

$$\begin{bmatrix} - & 0 & \frac{1}{2} & 0 & 0 \\ 0 & - & 0 & \frac{1}{3} & \frac{1}{3} \\ \frac{1}{2} & 0 & - & 0 & 0 \\ 0 & \frac{1}{3} & 0 & - & \frac{1}{3} \\ 0 & \frac{1}{3} & 0 & \frac{1}{3} & - \end{bmatrix}$$

Clearly, M3 deflates similarity by the size of category, on the reasoning that the more unusual co-occurrences, or the more fine discriminations, denote greater similarity.

Measure 4 (M4): Information-Theoretic (Burton's Z). This measure is quite different in form and content from the other Burton measures, since it also takes into account the pairs in *different* cells. It is akin to M3 in emphasizing the similarity of pairs from small categories and is based upon the information "surprisal value" (Attneave, 1959, p. 6) of each category.[31] This measure is defined in terms of two contributions: (1) the probability that two objects j and k will be found in the *same* category, a

$$p_a^i = n_a(n_a - 1)/N(N - 1)$$

where n_a is the number of objects in category a, and N is the total number of objects, and (2) the probability that j and k will be found in *different* categories:

$$Q^i = 1 - \sum_a p_a^i$$

The contribution that each pair of objects (j, k) makes is defined as its "surprisal" value, according to whether they are in the same or different groups:

$\log_2(p_a^i)$ if j and k are in the same group, and
$\log_2(Q^i)$ if j and k are in different groups.

Since surprisal is negatively related to the size of the group (the smaller the category, the higher the surprisal), this Z measure will (like M3) emphasize finer discriminations, but unlike M3 a negative quantity is added in when (j, k) are in different cells, hence making explicit allowance for pairs occurring in different categories.

In the present case, since the probability of two objects being in the same category is 0.1 for category I, and 0.3 for category II, and the probability for being in different categories is 0.6, the matrix of similarity (surprisal values) for the individual co-occurrence matrix corresponding to partition P would be:

$$
\begin{bmatrix}
- & 0.74 & 3.32 & 0.74 & 0.74 \\
0.74 & - & 0.74 & 1.74 & 1.74 \\
3.32 & 0.74 & - & 0.74 & 0.74 \\
0.74 & 1.74 & 0.74 & - & 1.74 \\
0.74 & 1.74 & 0.74 & 1.74 & -
\end{bmatrix}
$$

Suitably normalized (Burton, 1972, pp. 60–61), this quantity forms M4 (Burton's Z).

3.3.2. Dissociation Between Categories: Rosenberg's Measure

Rosenberg has pioneered the use of free-sorting data in social psychology and has been one of its most prolific users, especially as a tool in the study of personality trait relationships (Rosenberg et al., 1968; Rosenberg and Sedlack, 1972a, b; Rosenberg and Kim, 1975; Rosenberg and Cohen, 1977; Rosenberg, 1982). In this method, the subject is asked to describe one (or more) persons in terms of a set of traits (objects) provided by the researcher. There are two variants of this sorting exercise.

1. Each trait may be allocated to *only one* reference person so that in terms of the method of sorting, each reference person (RP) functions as a category (there are as many categories as reference persons), and the task can be interpreted as a free-sorting (if the number of RPs is not prespecified) or as a fixed-sorting (if the number of RPs is prespecified). In either event, the sorting constitutes a partition of mutually exclusive categories, and any leftover trait names are allocated as a residual group of singletons.
2. Each trait may be allocated freely between one or more RPs, so that the exercise turns into an overlapping categorization, and traits/objects may occur in more than one category. This variant is not a partition, and care must be exercised in the analysis of resulting data. [Wing and

Nelson (1972) discuss this variant and provide a dissimilarity measure for such overlapping data.]

A particularly imaginative way of using the method of sorting is Rosenberg's use of this approach to describe characters (RPs) in literary accounts by noting the trait-adjectives used by the author to describe them and then using a co-occurrence-based dissimilarity measure (described below) as a basis for a scaling representation (Rosenberg and Jones, 1972; Rosenberg, 1988).

Rosenberg also developed a measure of dissimilarity particularly adapted to the trait-sorting context (named "dissociation" in Rosenberg and Sedlak, 1972a), but in no way restricted to it. First, the "disagreement score" (s_{ij}) is calculated for each pair of traits (i, j) by counting the number of subjects who assign i and j to *different* categories/RPs—a sort of negative co-occurrence. For example, if in a sample of 100 individuals, 85 sort the traits *unsociable* and *pessimistic* together to describe the same RP, the disagreement score is $(100 - 85) = 15$. The overall measure of Rosenberg's disassociation (δ_{ij}) is defined as[32]:

$$\delta_{ij} = \sum_{k \in T} \left(s_{ik} - s_{jk} \right)^2$$

where T is the set of traits. Rosenberg and Sedlak (1972a, p. 142) explain and justify it as follows:

The main rationale for using the δ-measure ... rather than the s-measure is that the δ-measure 'contains' the s-measure of direct trait co-occurrence *plus* a measure for indirect trait co-occurrence. An indirect trait co-occurrence for any two traits i and j refers to an instance in which i and k co-occur in one description, j and k co-occur in another description, and i and j do not occur in either description.

In this, Rosenberg's δ-measure resembles Burton's M4 measure by taking account of the categories in which two objects do not occur, as well as those in which they do. An extensive analysis of the behavior and properties of the δ-measure has been made by Drasgow and Jones (1979), who argue that the inclusion of indirect dissimilarities not only regains information about finer distinctions (at least in the square-root version of the δ-measure), but also leads to better fitting and more interpretable multidimensional scaling solutions. [The methodology and conclusions have been questioned in turn by Van der Kloot and van Hert (1991), but without seriously subverting the main conclusions.]

3.3.3. Multiple Co-Occurrences

It has been argued that simply taking the pairwise information out of sorting to use as a basis for the similarity measure distorts important structural information and that in particular it allows quite different sets of sortings to be represented by the same pairwise co-occurrence matrix. Daws (1996), following Hubert and Arabie (1985), proposes using *triple* co-occurrences to ameliorate the situation and develops a statistic that measures the similarity of each triple, corrected for the similarities of the three corresponding pairs:

$$s^*_{abc} = s_{abc} - C_N(s_{ab} + s_{ac} + s_{bc})$$

The correction factor C_N acts as a weight, based on the Bell Number of total possible number of partitions (Moser and Wyman, 1955), that becomes smaller as the number of objects becomes large. A more direct approach to the yet more general case of n-tuples (representing information on the dissimilarity between co-occurring pairs, triples, quadruples, ...) has been proposed by Cox et al. (1991), with some success.

A radically different approach is taken by Bimler and Kirkland (1997, 1998), who view the (necessary) transitivity of ordinary co-occurrence data as potentially misleading[33] and have developed a method of "reconstructed dyads" to take account of this.

3.4. An Example

In the Occupational Cognition Project, 71 respondents free-sorted the set of 32 occupational titles (OTs) and another 66 sorted the set of 50 occupational descriptions (ODs). Forty-one of those who had sorted the occupational descriptions went on to sort the occupational titles as instances into their earlier-formed groups of occupational descriptions, thus producing sortings of 82 objects. The two basic characteristics—the number of categories formed, and the size of the

TABLE 2

Occupations Data: Number of Groups

	Number of Groups	Number of Nonsingleton Groups	Size of Largest Group
32 occupational titles	2–13 6.78 (2.60)	2–10 6.06 (2.07)	4–21 9.49 (3.66)
52 occupational descriptions	3–29 7.77 (4.96)	2–10 4.90 (1.57)	7–30 16.54 (4.83)

Entries in each cell are the range, followed by the mean and standard deviation.

largest group—are given in Table 2 (Coxon and Jones, 1979b, U2.4, pp. 161–163).

It might be thought that the number of groups a person forms would be positively related to the number of objects presented, but things are somewhat more complicated. In fact, the number of groups formed is very similar for both sets, and although the average number of groups is marginally higher for occupational descriptions, this is reversed when singleton groups are ignored. The importance of ignoring singleton groups is emphasized when the corresponding standard deviations are compared: the dispersion in the number of groups certainly decreases for titles, but it decreases very dramatically for descriptions, reflecting the fact that in the set of descriptions there are many which do not readily fit in the subjects' categorizations. It is also worth commenting that the average number of categories formed in this study is smaller than those reported for other domains,[34] but surprisingly close to Miller (1956)'s "Magic Number 7 ± 2," the number of reliable distinctions observed for many simple domains and attributes.

The distribution of the height of the sortings (normalized because of the difference in numbers between the two sets) is presented in Figure 8. Now the relative differences are more apparent: the less concrete descriptions have a somewhat higher (and more dispersed) "lumpiness" than the titles, but the similarities are still marked.

When the distribution of PAIRBONDS and APPROX dissimilarity measures between subjects' sortings of the OTs and ODs is examined (Coxon and Jones, 1979a, p. 34), it is noticeable, once again, how very similar the sortings of OTs really are compared to ODs, not only in the sense that the average normalized PAIRBONDS similarity between sortings is virtually identical. On average, 25% (126/496) of a subject's pairs would need to be shifted to change one subject's OTs

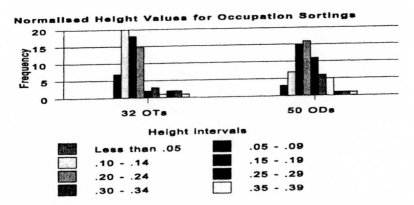

Figure 8. Normalized height values for occupational sortings. Occupational titles: $N = 71$; mean = 0.18; SD = 0.10; occupational descriptions: $N = 66$; mean = 0.24; SD = 0.19.

sorting into another one and 30% (366/1225) between two OD sortings.

An inspection of intersecting pairs of sortings also produced interesting results (Coxon and Jones, 1979a, pp. 29–33). Two examples are given in Figure 9. These two subjects produce what is on any account two highly similar sortings; they agree in allocating all but three occupational titles: Male Psychiatric Nurse, Bank Clerk, and Policemen. The bases used for the sortings—in effect, educational level and income—provide a nice example of concordance between the "scientific" and "folk" accounts of social status, for it is precisely these variables that best predict occupational prestige scores (Reiss et al., 1961, pp. 196 et seq; Coxon and Jones, 1979a, pp. 10–23). The normalized PAIRBONDS (dissimilarity) value between these two sortings is 0.18 and the Rand (similarity) Index is 0.83, denoting what is by any account a high degree of agreement, and one of the highest found in the Project. In terms of the quantities defined in Appendix 3 on website to characterize the types of agreement and disagreement in the allocation of the 496 pairs, the subjects

- agree that 41% of the pairs should be allocated to the same class (type I).
- agree that 42% should be allocated to different classes (type II) (hence they are in 83% agreement).

A: Intersection matrix between Y035 and G292

	G292	(Chartered accountant)
Y035 (Decor Adviser)	*A: Further education not required*	*B: Formal education required*
I: Low potential salary	GM BM C AD PL UMO PHT BSL RCK RED PO TDH TDR BC	
II: High potential salary	MPN BCK PM	CA SST ST SW CPR MOR PST CE AP A GEO SMG ESG NJ LT

B: Full intersection table, including marginals

	G292	(Chartered accountant)	(Sums)
Y035 (Decor Adviser)	*A: Further education not required*	*B: Formal education required*	
I: Low potential salary	14	0	14
II: High potential salary	3	15	18
(Sums)	17	15	$n = 32$

n.b.: Y035's category I is a proper subset of G292's category A
G292's category B is a proper subset of Y035's category II

Figure 9. Intersection between two subject's sortings. Rand Index = 0.83.

- disagree on 8% of the pairs, putting them in the same class in one sorting (Y035) and in different classes in the other (G292).
- disagree on 9% of the pairs, putting them in different classes in one sorting (Y035) and in the same class in the other (G292). (Hence they are in 17% disagreement.)

Finally, the co-occurrence matrix was calculated from these data and is reproduced in Figure 7.

4. ANALYZING SORTING DATA

Once sorting data are collected and subjected to preliminary examination, several decisions concerning the analysis face the researcher:

- to find a "collective representation" of the objects, or
- to examine how individuals differ in their sorting behavior, or
- to represent both objects and individuals in the same representation, or
- to examine patterns of divergence from a "collective representation" of the sortings.

Any of these issues can be dealt with using the growing range of models available in what has come to be called "combinatorial data analysis" (CDA) (Arabie and Hubert, 1992; Arabie et al., 1996), concerned primarily with

> the location of arrangements that are optimal for the representation of a given data set ... or with trying to determine in a confirmatory manner whether a specific object arrangement given *a priori* reflects the observed data (Arabie and Hubert, 1992, p. 170).

This approach (CDA) covers modes of analysis such as discrete models of clustering and fitting tree-structures as well as multidimensional scaling, and it stays considerably closer to the data than more conventional approaches.

To exploit these models, we need first to consider the general issue of how to represent sortings and then go on to characterize them in terms of the Coombsian theory of data (Coombs, 1964; Jacoby, 1991) as extended by Carroll and Arabie (1980). We can then examine the kind of models available for data representation and the transformations or levels of measurement assumed by the models.

4.1. Representing Sortings

As they stand, sortings are a classic instance of a nominal scale: an exclusive and exhaustive set of categories, which constitutes a partition of the objects. As data, the question of representing sortings begins from two basic assumptions: (1) that all objects in the same category are considered to have a higher similarity to each other than they do to the other objects and (2) that the categories themselves are considered to be maximally distinct and separated. The purpose of analysis is then to represent a set of such sortings by means of one (or more) model in such a way that the resulting representation is as close as possible to the original data and displays significant aspects of their structure.

At an elementary level, the first thing is to find out where agreement about the structure of a partition is highest, since on some aspects there will be perfect agreement and on others there will be disagreement; indeed, it is often the case that people agree a lot more about what *does not* go together than on what does.

But how can one obtain a single representation of "the" sorting, when disagreement exists? Many attempts to define consensus in sorting (and in trees) have sought to define rules that a consensus structure should have, such as the "median approach," which defines a metric (such as the D or PAIRBONDS metric) between the partitions and then finds a partition—the best-fitting median partition—such that the sum of distances from it to the partitions is minimized. Although some progress has been made in the enterprise of calculating such a partition using linear programming approaches (Barthélemy and Monjardet, 1988; Day, 1988), a serious attempt to explore all possible partitions of a given size in the search for an optimal one is doomed to practical failure, given the astronomical numbers involved,[35] so it is not a feasible procedure for large data sets.[36]

A rather different, but more feasible, procedure for assessing the degree of consensus in sorting is a technique developed in anthropology (but with strong reliance on Psychological Test Theory) called "consensus analysis" (Romney et al., 1986). This statistical method both estimates the degree of agreement among the respondents in their assessment of the similarity of the objects in a domain and also infers the "culturally correct" answer to items. It works from three assumptions:

1. *"Common truth"* or *"one culture"*: Each item has one (culturally) correct answer; therefore, there is a common culture shared by all and there are no systematically different subcultural perspectives.

2. *Local independence*: If a subject does not know the correct "answer" he guesses randomly and does so independently of all other subjects.

3. *Homogeneity of items/cultural competence*: Questions are all within the same coherent domain, and items are of the same "difficulty" level. This is a strong assumption, but can be interpreted as meaning that if a subject is competent in a given domain, he will be equally competent in answering all the constituent items however much he may be incompetent in other domains.

Cultural consensus analysis is based on defining the similarity between pairs of subjects in terms of the cross-product (correlation) of their scores, using a least-squares principal axes variant of factor analysis (Lewis-Beck, 1994) known as the minimum residual method (Comrey, 1962) to obtain estimates of each subject's "cultural competence." According to the assumptions of the model (especially assumption 1), the solution should be dominated by the first eigenvalue (latent root), representing cultural consensus or competence, and other roots should be small by comparison. A rough measure for this requirement is that the ratio of the first root to the second should be not less than 2 or 3.

While this procedure has something of a rough and ready statistical feel to it, it is often used to assess the extent of agreement or consensus among subjects before proceeding to analysis of the data (Maiolo et al., 1993), and it is implemented as an option in the ANTHROPAC package.

4.1.1. Observations and Data

In data theory, a distinction is conventionally made between the "observations," in effect, the raw data, like the actual sortings themselves, and the "data," which consist of these observations interpreted by the investigator in a particular way.

The "shape" of data concerns primarily their *way* and their *mode*. The "way" of the data refers to the dimensionality of the array of observations:

- one-way data consist of a single row/column (a vector),
- two-way data consist of rows and columns (a matrix), and
- three-way data consist of a set or stack of matrices forming a "cube."

The observations derived from sorting are interpreted primarily as two-way, namely the basic preferred data format (PDF) data matrix, representing individuals (rows) and objects/stimuli (columns). But there may also be replications of the basic two-way data matrix, (different occasions, times, samples, measures), making it in this case a three-way matrix, consisting of a "cube" of data or a "stack" of two-way data.

Once the way of the data is determined, the question arises about whether to represent both individuals and objects jointly or each type singly. The *mode* of the data refers to the number of distinct sets of entities that are to be represented. In the case of sorting data:

- *two-way, one-mode* data will consist of either the $p \times p$ matrix of dis/similarities between the *objects* or the $N \times N$ matrix of dis/similarities between the *sortings* or individuals.

- *two-way, two-mode* PDF data will consist of the basic data matrix, where the rows refer to individual sortings, the columns to the objects, and the entries give the category-number into which individual i sorts object j.

For sortings data, the third way is especially relevant if the researcher uses different proximity measures (as when several Arabie-Boorman measures are used on the same data set) or different occasions/times [as in the nightly co-dormition time series of the vervet monkeys (Struhsaker, 1967)]. Then, as for two-way data, there are variants based on different modes:

- *three-way, two-mode* data will consist of a "stack" (one mode) of square matrices (the other mode) referring either to objects or to individuals.

- *three-way, three-mode* data where there is a joint mapping of individuals and objects for each slice of the data cube.

The types of data and choices for analysis of sortings can be summarized as shown in Figure 10. The organization of the figure emphasizes that the analysis process consists of a series of choices—first about how to interpret the data and then about the model (and scaling transformation) that is appropriate. Only then is the choice of computer program to implement the analysis realistically made.

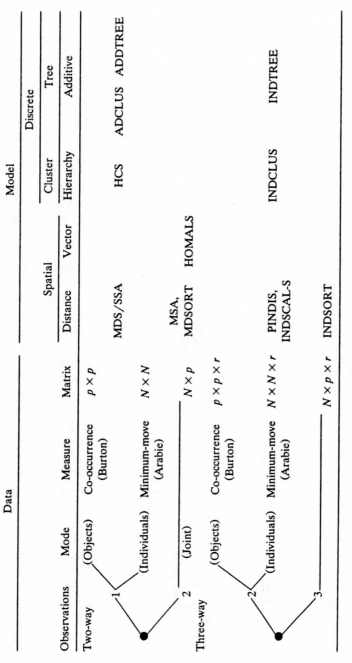

Figure 10. Data type and models for the analysis of sortings and derived data.

4.1.2. Models

The basic divergence among models for representing sortings data is between spatial and discrete models.

4.1.2.1. Spatial Models. The most crucial characteristic of space is that it is dimensional and it is continuous. The two main variants of spatial models are the *distance* model, often known as "smallest space analysis" and the *vector* model, of which correspondence analysis and factor analysis are commonly used instances. In both, the objects (or subjects) are represented as points, and it is the mode of the representation of similarity that differentiates them—the distance model maps similarity as proximity (and hence dissimilarity as distance), and the vector model maps similarity as the angular separation between the points considered as vectors drawn from the centre of the space.

The appropriate family of models to implement the *distance* models exist within multidimensional scaling (MDS), and these models are very extensively used for representing sortings data. MDS has been succinctly described in two books in this series (Kruskal and Wish, 1978; Arabie et al., 1987) and is more extensively documented in a number of other texts (Schiffman et al., 1981; Coxon, 1982; Green et al., 1989; Cox and Cox, 1994; Borg and Groenen, 1997). Developments in the area of scaling and distance models have been regularly summarized (Carroll and Arabie, 1980; Arabie and Carroll, 1998). It will be assumed here that the reader is familiar with the basic nonmetric MDS distance models so that attention can be focused on those variants most appropriate to sortings data.

Among scalar-product models, factor analysis is the most commonly used variant, especially among Q methodologists (McKeown and Thomas, 1988) who use fixed-sorting methods to produce ranking scores and then correlate and factor them.

Correspondence analysis (CA) (Weller and Romney, 1990; Greenacre, 1993) analyzes a *table* of frequencies to obtain a visual representation of the similarity within the r row categories and within the c column categories of the table. This is done so that the categories that are closely related to each other are also close in the resulting plot. Simple correspondence analysis (SCA) actually works not on the table frequencies themselves but upon the row-percentaged profiles of the row categories, and a "chi-square distance" is calculated between them.[37] The frequencies are first turned into proportions, and then their expected value (under the assumption of statistical independence) is subtracted. The resulting quantity (the numerator of the equation below) is standardized by the geometric mean of the marginal probabilities:

$$\frac{p_{ij} - p_i p_j}{\sqrt{p_i} \sqrt{p_j}}$$

Simple correspondence analysis performs a singular value decomposition (SVD) (Weller and Romney, 1990) of these chi-square residuals and thus derives both the optimal scores (or "loadings") associated with the row categories and those associated with the column categories. The first two (largest) principal components of the solution are normally retained and the row and column categories are plotted as two sets of points in this two-dimensional space, yielding a visual representation of the similarity between the categories.[38] A generalization of simple correspondence analysis named multiple correspondence analysis (or homogeneity analysis), portraying both objects and categories, is particularly relevant to analyzing sorting data and is discussed in Section 4.2.3.2 below.

4.1.2.2. Discrete Models. Discrete models have an obvious affinity with classification and sorting. The basic structure represented in a discrete model is the *category*, however named—class, cluster, subset, group, taxon—and the most common representations used in discrete models are clustering structures and tree or network structures.

4.1.2.3. Clustering. Cluster analysis, under various names, is an extensive and well-explored area with a large bibliography. Originating in numerical taxonomy (Sokal and Sneath, 1963; Jardine and Sibson, 1971), classification and/or clustering has spread rapidly into a wide range of other disciplines and has its own *Journal of Classification*. The field is well reviewed in Cormack (1971) and is given a practical exposition in a number of texts (Everitt, 1993; Gordon, 1981; Aldenderfer and Blashfield, 1984; Bailey, 1994), as well as in a now dated but important and provocatively titled paper (Ball, 1965). Important recent papers are collected in Arabie et al. (1996).

The area of clustering has been divided down by Cormack (1971, p. 321) into three types:

1. *Partitioning*, where the objects are divided into a set of classes or clusters, which are required to be mutually exclusive and exhaustive.
2. *Hierarchical classification*, where there is a nested set of partitions, each of which forms a separate level. Each higher level is a coarser generalization of those beneath it. The nested levels are often represented as a tree.
3. *Clumping* (or additive clustering), in which the clusters/classes can overlap.

Cormack's distinctions are used here, and only the variants commonly used for analyzing sorting are mentioned at this point.

The simplest approach to *partition clustering*[39] is known as *k-means clustering* (Ball, 1965; MacQueen, 1967), which seeks a single partition containing a given number (k) of categories (specified by the user) and then iteratively moves objects between categories, until a (possibly local) minimum within-category sum of squares is reached.[40] This is then "the" solution—a statistically simple and computationally fairly straightforward procedure—but, of course, one that may well not correspond to any subject's sorting.

The *hierarchical clustering scheme*[41] (HCS) is a more complex variant of clustering. Although metric variants are available, the most commonly used version is nonmetric HCS (Johnson, 1967). As a procedure, HCS usually operates from pairwise proximity coefficients and presents the solution as a *set* of related partitions, typically from the partition where each element is in its own cluster (the splitter) to the partition where all the elements are in the one category (the lumper). The partitions of the solution are nested in a hierarchical manner so that the partition at each level is more fine than the one above it. Consequently each level is related to the next by a union (upwards) and an intersection (downwards).

The process of constructing a hierarchical clustering from a perfect set of data (defined by the ultrametric inequality, see Appendix 2B on website) is illustrated in Figure 11. The procedure starts from a matrix of data dis/similarities and at this stage, each point is considered to form its own cluster (the splitter stage). The first step consists of identifying the most similar (least dissimilar) pair of objects from the matrix—here C and D—and merges them into a cluster of two

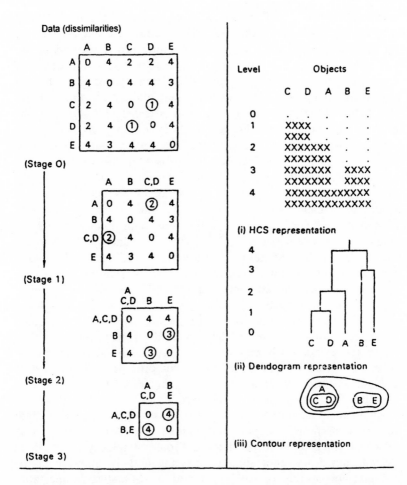

Figure 11. Construction of an hierarchical clustering scheme (perfect data). (From Coxon, 1982, p. 101.)

points, which from this point on are treated as a single object. The data matrix is reduced, removing the rows/columns for points C and D and replacing them by a row and column for cluster {C, D}. The issue now arises about how to define the distance between the *cluster* {C, D} and each of the remaining points, i.e., $\delta(\{C, D\}, x)$. In these data, the dissimilarity between C and other points is the same as the distance between D and the other points, and there is no problem in defining the distance between the cluster and the other points. But for imperfect data, which do not satisfy the ultrametric inequality, this will not be the case and some way must be found to choose the distance from among the (normally) different values given by the constituent points in the cluster. Various alternatives are possible (the SPSS Clustering command menu lists eight), and each alternative in effect defines a distinct method and may give rise to a different solution. Since the identification of an acceptable collective representation of the subjects' categories is a critical issue in analyzing sortings, the choice must be deliberate. Johnson himself suggests that the two extreme possibilities be considered, so that the extent of variation is made clear: one where the *smallest* of the distances ("nearest neighbor," also called the minimum, connectedness, or single linkage) is consistently taken as "the" distance, and one where the *largest* of the distances ("furthest neighbor," also called maximum, diameter, or complete linkage) is taken. Only in the case of perfect data will the two extreme methods give rise to identical solutions; normally there will be considerable differences. It is always advisable, therefore, to perform both the solutions on the same data set to get a clear idea of just how much divergence there is.[42] If a single representation is required, it is prudent to either choose the more interpretable solution or run a compromise solution such as median clustering, which at each stage simply takes the median value to define the distance between clusters.

Clumping or additive (or overlapping) clustering is a further variant of simple clustering (Shepard and Arabie, 1979; Arabie and Carroll, 1980a). It is a combinatorial method of some complexity[43] and differs dramatically from other simple clustering both by allowing in the solution for overlap of categories and in estimating "importance weights" for each category (or "property" as the documentation puts it). The form of the additive cluster model is as follows:

$$s_{ij} \approx \sum_k w_k p_{ik} p_{jk} + c$$

where $p_{ik} = 1$ if object i is in cluster k, and is 0 otherwise, $p_{jk} = 1$ if object j is in cluster k, and is 0 otherwise, w_k is the (nonnegative) weight of cluster k, and c is the additive constant.

In the additive clustering model, the similarity between a pair of objects/subjects is represented as the sum of the weights ("salience" or "importance" or "elevation") of the clusters in which they belong, and the model simply states that "the predicted similarity of stimuli is equal to the sum of the numerical weights of the subsets containing both of those stimuli (plus an additive constant)" (Arabie and Carroll, 1980b, p. 3). If both objects i and j are allocated to a single cluster (i.e., share the same property k), then $p_{ik} p_{jk} = 1$ and the weight w_k applies, but if either or both lie outside the cluster, the product is 0, and the weight does not apply. Consequently the similarity value equals the sum of the weights of just those clusters to which an object applies and the weights w_k only contribute to the similarity of those objects that possess it. The additive constant can be thought of as the weight of the "universal set," i.e., a separate cluster representing all the objects in the set.

Additive clustering is therefore a discrete representation of the data as a collection of (possibly overlapping) clusters or "categories." The estimation of the model is implemented using an algorithm known as MAPCLUS (Carroll and Arabie, 1980), which takes the user's estimation of the number of clusters, and then proceeds to estimate cluster membership, estimate the cluster weights, and maximize the variance accounted for (VAF).[44]

An additive clustering scheme is a very powerful way of conceiving the structure underlying the data and is unique in representing overlap and in accounting for differential salience of categories. An example of an application of additive clustering and its representation in a MDS space is given in Figure 12, showing both the hierarchical clustering and an additive clustering of a co-occurrence matrix derived from a free-sorting of 20 body parts as reported in Miller (1969).

The numerical weight of the additive clusters is given in Figure 12A. The ADCLUS solution is embedded in a City-block metric MDS solution to the same data, and the numerical weights have been replaced by their ordinal number in Figure 12B in order to simplify presentation.

4.1.2.4. Discrete Representations: Trees. A rather different representation is given by the similarity tree model (DeSoete and Carroll, 1996; Corter, 1996). A tree is a graph consisting of arbitrarily located points (objects) linked by (undirected) arcs, where no points are

66

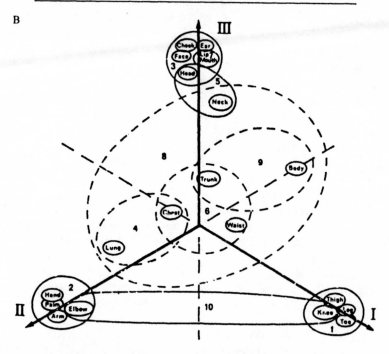

A

ORDINAL RANK	WEIGHT	ELEMENTS OF SUBSET
1	.820	knee, leg, thigh, toe
2	.754	arm, elbow, hand, palm
3	.722	ear, cheek, face, head, lip, mouth
4	.433	chest, lung
5	.348	head, neck
6	.315	chest, trunk, waist
7	.231	lip, mouth
8	.206	body, chest, lung, neck, trunk, waist
9	.204	body, trunk
10	.119	elbow, knee

B

Figure 12. ADCLUS: parts of body. A. ADCLUS solution to Miller (1969) body-parts sorting co-occurrences data. (Variance accounted for = 95.6% with 10 subsets, plus additive constant of .048). B. 10 ADCLUS weighted subsets embedded in a two-dimensional projection of a three-dimensional multidimensional City-block metric scaling of the same data. (From Shepard and Arabie, 1979, p. 115 (Figure 7), p. 16 (Table 9). Copyright © 1979 by the American Psychological Association. Reprinted with permission.)

isolates (hence all points are reachable or connected) and where there are no cycles. In the additive tree, each link has a value (its length) and the similarity between objects/subjects is represented as the sum of the shortest path between them.

There are two variants of the additive tree, the *hierarchical tree*, and the more general *additive tree*. Both variants of the additive tree satisfy the so-called four-point (Buneman) condition, defined in Appendix 2D on website, which is a generalization of the ultrametric inequality.

1. In the *hierarchical additive tree*, the representation is exactly like an HCS, except that the branches have values ("saliences"), and the similarity between two points is represented by the sum of the branch lengths from the root of the tree to the point that is their common ancestor (or *lub*: least upper bound). The path lengths have various interpretations, but an especially attractive one is due to the common features model of similarity (Tversky, 1977; Corter and Tversky, 1986): that the link weights reflect the salience or importance of the set of features that are shared by all the objects in the branch of that tree.

2. More common and less restrictive, the *additive tree* is represented not as a hierarchical structure, but as a graph. The difference in appearance is that the root of the additive tree is arbitrary, and similar, as Corter and Tversky point out (1986, p. 21), to the issue of choosing an appropriate rotation in factor analysis. Once again, the similarity between two objects is the sum of the lengths of the links between them.

4.1.3. Transformations

Transformations refer to the level of measurement assumed (or demonstrated) for the data. Once decided, this determines what information may legitimately be used in obtaining a solution to the data according to a particular model. Thus, the basic nonmetric MDS model seeks an ordinal rescaling from the original data dissimilarities into best-fitting metric quantities representing distances in a Euclidean space. Similarly, Johnson's HCS seeks an ordinal mapping into a set of "distances" satisfying the ultrametric inequality.

Although of major conceptual and practical importance in the 1960s and 1970s, the distinction between nonmetric (ordinal) scaling and metric (linear) scaling has in recent times become a good deal less salient. While it is often wisest to err on the side of caution and seek—at least initially—a monotonic (ordinal) rescaling of the data, this is often unnecessary or impossible if a nonmetric variant has not been developed. It is not uncommon to encounter solutions that are actually "quasi-nonmetric" in the sense that a metric solution is first obtained (often the easier and quicker option), and then a second stage was begun, which moved iteratively to satisfy ordinal constraints. But generally speaking, metric solutions have turned out to be surprisingly robust.

4.2. Two-Way Analysis

We turn now to the specifics of data analysis of sorting. The first major choice is whether to opt for a direct (joint) solution and represent both modes of the data or to aggregate over one mode and concentrate one mode—either the objects or the individual sorting. The usual choice is to opt first for the two-way, *one-mode*, analysis; the objects and the categories of the sorting are treated quite independently and are given separate consideration. The researcher decides to concentrate either on the similarity between the p objects or upon the similarity between the N subjects' sortings.

4.2.1. Two-Way, One-Mode Data: Comparing the Objects

Usually, the relationships between the p objects of the sorting are considered first, and a co-occurrence (similarity) matrix is formed, based on the frequency with which two (or more) objects are present in the same category among the individual sortings. That done, multidimensional scaling is used to locate the object points in conformity to the proximity data, and, secondly, hierarchical clustering is used on the same data to delineate the category boundaries round the located points. The hierarchical clusters are then drawn into the MDS configuration as concentric contours—representing category boundaries of increasing inclusion—round the constituent points of each cluster.

By far the most commonly used similarity measure used as input to analysis programs is the direct frequency count (Miller's co-occurrence measure, M1 above, Section 3.3.1), followed by the two measures that take both the same and different categories into account: the Rosenberg δ-measure and Burton's Z co-occurrence measures (M4 above, Section 3.3.1).

The scaling behavior of M1 to M4 has not been systematically investigated, but the results from Burton himself (Burton, 1975;

Burton and Romney, 1975) and from Coxon and Jones (1979b, pp. 173–178) show strong similarities, independent of the dimensionality of the solution and of the size and nature of objects, as is seen in Figure 13.

This figure summarizes the rank-order of the stress$_1$ values reported for a total of four free-sorting data sets using the Burton measures. Within each data set, the same rank-order of stress$_1$ values for the measures holds for solutions in different dimensions. Coxon and Jones report solutions[45] in dimensions 5 to 1 and Burton for dimensions 2 and 3.

The similarity is striking; both M1 and M2 produce relatively lower stress$_1$ values than M3 and M4, probably because M1 and M2 are bound to produce somewhat more clustered solutions emphasizing, as they do, the grosser characteristics. Where data exist, M3 seems to produce the worst-fit solution. However, M4 produces more interpretable solutions, in the sense that they conform more closely to the original (unaggregated data), and probably because, alone among the Burton measures, information about indirect links is taken into account. Multidimensional scaling solutions of the four Burton mea-

Domain	Ranking of Stress$_1$ Values	Dim's	Reference
50 occupational descriptions plus 32 occupational titles	M1 < M2 < M4 < M3	V → I	Coxon and Jones, 1979b, p. 175
32 occupational titles	M2 < M1 < M4 < M3	V → I	Coxon and Jones, 1979b, p. 173
34 occupational titles	M2 < M1 < M4	III, II	Burton, 1975, p. 417
34 behaviors	M2 < M1 < M4	III, II	Burton, 1975, p. 417

Notes:
Measures: M1 = Miller's F; M2 = Burton's G; (M3 = Burton's un-named measure); M4 = Burton's Z.
Burton does not report analysis using M3.

Figure 13. Stress rankings of Burton measures.

sures on the same set of sortings of 32 occupational titles by 71 subjects is reproduced in Section 4.4.

A generally useful utility for interpreting such configurations or for combining sorting with ratings of the same object is to position such information in the space as a vector. This procedure is known as "external property-fitting" (PRO-FIT, Carroll and Chang, 1968). It orients the vector as a direction in the space in which the property is increasing. It is available in several packages[46] (see Appendix 4), and together with hierarchical clustering, property-fitting is the most common method for interpreting a smallest-space configuration (Coxon, 1982, pp. 93–116).

4.2.2. Two-Way, One-Mode Data: Comparing Individuals' Sortings

Individual sortings are compared using one (or more) of the Arabie-Boorman measures described in Section 3.2.2. Each measure produces a $N \times N$ matrix of coefficients. In this section, attention is restricted to the PAIRBONDS and APPROX measures. As in the case of the objects, the most obvious step after calculating the chosen measure(s) is to scale the data, using a nonmetric distance model and/or a cluster analysis. But before the scaling or clustering of Arabie measures is done, an important admonitory tale needs to be told.

Arabie and Boorman (1973) investigated the scaling behavior of their 12 measures, with some surprising results. The sortings "data" they used consisted of all the partitions for 4, 5, 6, and 10 points (with and without lumper and splitter partitions, and using random subsets for 6 and 10 points, due to the huge number of partitions involved[47]). Then 12 measures were calculated for each set of partitions, and a nonmetric distance model[48] multidimensional scaling was performed in two dimensions for each measure. The solutions were rotated into maximum (Procrustean) concordance to a target configuration.

Summarizing a complex and extended discussion: certain important results that are highly relevant for our purposes are as follows.

1. Hierarchical cluster analysis, which is of course designed to detect clusterings of points that are in close proximity, repeatedly, and in both variants, produced results that "were typically degenerate in the sense that clusterings were weak and uninterpretable" (Arabie and Boorman, 1973, p. 163). HCS (and any other clustering procedure dependent on

proximity values) is therefore not recommended for representing Arabie measures of sortings data.

2. When scaled, the structural information about differences between partitions is represented in two quite different ways by different measures. *Neither* form of representation corresponds to the conventional ways of interpreting MDS solutions in terms of regions of higher and lower density (Coxon, 1982, pp. 93–116). These two forms consist of a *contour* representation and a *linear* representation, which are associated with the PAIRBONDS and the APPROX measures, respectively.

3. In the case of the PAIRBONDS (height) measure the two-dimensional[49] scaling of individual sortings of a given height maps into a set of concentric circles, centred upon the "splitter" (Figure 14A). Each circle links the subjects who have sortings of the same height value, and the radial distance of the circles from the splitter (at the center) is in proportion to the height value of the sorting concerned.

There is clearly good recovery of the lattice types as contour lines in the scaling representation. The [MDS] algorithm behaves much as though $P_{splitter}$ and P_{lumper} were opposing attractors, each trying to organize the types around itself as circular isosimilarity contours (Coxon and Jones, 1979a, pp. 86–90).

Consequently, if the MDS configuration resulting from a PAIRBONDS measure were to be interpreted in terms of the clustering or proximity of individual points then the height information is entirely lost, inferences drawn will be in error, and the crucial structural information will be overlooked. When applied to actual sortings data, the same contour structure can usually be perceived, but the subject points will only occur for partitions present in the data (see Figure 17). To make the contours clear, the points should be labeled by their height value and points of the same value joined by a circle or by a sector of a circle. That done, the splitter and the lumper (or the nearest approximation in the data to them) can be located, the splitter probably near the center of the contours and the lumper at the periphery. When these two points are joined, they form the "lumper/splitter axis." It will also be possible to get some idea of the distribution of the height value of the partitions.

4. In the case of APPROX (and some other measures), the data necessarily contain a large number of ties. Now, however, the scaling representation is quite different to the PAIRBONDS contour representation.

72

A

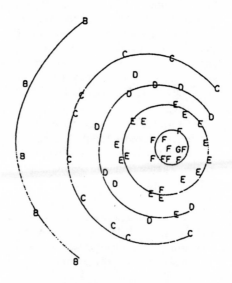

B   Partition Isomorphism Types for the 5-lattice

Type	Number of distinct partitions having that type	Code	Height $(D(P))$ in Table IV)
5	1	A	10
4-1	5	B	6
3-2	10	C	4
3-1-1	10	D	3
2-2-1	15	E	2
2-1-1-1	10	F	1
1-1-1-1-1	1	G	0

Figure 14. A. Scaling of PAIRBONDS on 5-lattice with both endpoints present. Two dimensions, Euclidean metric, L-configuration. Stress formula $1 = 23.9\%$. The points are labeled by type according to the coding in the table. B. Partition types. (From Arabie and Boorman, 1973, p. 162 (Table VII and Figure 1). Reprinted with permission.)

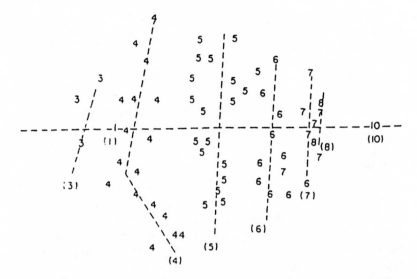

Figure 15. Scaling of APPROX on 10-lattice sample with both endpoints present. Two dimensions, Euclidean metric, random initial configuration. Stress formula 1 = 19.1%. Points are labeled by the cardinality $|P|$ of the number of categories in the corresponding partition. Numbers in parentheses classify components of the plot by the cardinality of the partitions that they contain. (From Arabie and Boorman, 1973, p. 175 (Figure 10). Reprinted with permission.)

APPROX scaling configurations by contrast are arrayed in linear segments dividing up the lumper-splitter axis (Figure 15). Each segment represents the cardinality (number) of the partitions they contain. Again, this linear structure will not be detected by proximity-based analysis methods.

5. Inclusion of the extreme (lumper/splitter) points is advisable to ensure the full representation of the structure in the configuration and even to avoid degenerate solutions.

6. Strong (as opposed to weak) normalization of a basic measure tends to turn the scaling solution structure inside out. This is particularly striking for the strong normalization $(1 - NT/1 + 2)$ of the PAIRBONDS measure, whose scaling solution centers the concentric circles of sortings points on the lumper, and the height values decrease systematically (p. 173), unlike the PAIRBONDS representation centered on the splitter with the circles increasing in height value.

In consequence, it is important to know how a given measure behaves in a MDS representation before interpreting it—typically as a concentric contours of height value in the case of PAIRBONDS or as a linear segment of the cardinality of the partition in the case of APPROX.

An example of the scaling of the PAIRBONDS measure of the 71 individual sortings of 32 occupational titles is presented in Figure 17.

4.2.3. Two-Way, Two-Mode Data: Objects and Categories

A main shortcoming of the forms of analysis so far is that only one mode is represented, and there is no relation between the object/stimuli space and the subject/data source solutions. In each case, information on the other mode has been washed out in aggregation, and the solutions for the objects and for the individuals, whether discrete or spatial, are not directly comparable and cannot in any simple sense be related to each other. Moreover, there is no representation of the subjects' categories in either solution.

In two-mode analysis, by contrast, both the objects *and the categories* are represented, although individuals as such are not represented directly until three-way analysis is used. The three models which follow—Takane's MDSORT, the Leiden/SPSS HOMALS, and the Guttman-Lingoes multidimensional scalogram analysis (MSA)—have certain strong similarities, and they will often yield similar solutions. Both work directly from the $N \times p$ sorting data rather than from derived dis/similarities and represent the objects directly in the graphical solution. Moreover, they all represent the subjects' categories, although indirectly in Takane's model. The methods used to achieve the optimum solution are also similar, using dual or optimal scaling techniques (to quantify the locations of the points).[50]

4.2.3.1. Takane's MDSORT Model.

The model implemented in a program named MDSORT (Takane, 1981b, c) is designed specifically for the direct analysis of sorting data. Because of its particular relevance and importance, this model needs more detailed consideration than most. Readers uninterested in the derivation should move to the next section.

In the traditions of optimal scaling and quantification analysis, Takane (1980) developed MDSORT as a joint representation of objects and subjects' categories, which simultaneously scales and represents the sorting data. Takane's model takes the data in PDF, as a matrix F consisting of a set of N row vectors, one for each respondent i, arrayed so that each column refers to a given object j and where the entry $f(i, j)$ consists of the category/group number in which the object is located. The categories are in a sequential (but arbitrary) numbering. That is:

$$F = \left[f_{ij} \right], \qquad (i = 1, \ldots, N; j = 1, \ldots, p)$$

where the value of the cell f_{ij} is the category number (say, k) in which object j occurs in i's sorting.

This F data matrix is now expanded into a *set* of individual matrices, G_k, each matrix k being of size p rows and q categories (*n.b.* q will differ from subject to subject in free-sorting, but will be the same number for fixed-sorting):

$$G_k = \left[g_{jq}^{(k)} \right], \qquad (i = 1, \ldots, N; j = 1, \ldots, p; q = \#c^i)$$

where

$g_{jq}^{(k)} = 1, 0$: 1 if object j occurs in subject i's qth category;

0 otherwise.

Takane (1980) proceeds directly to a joint scaling by decomposing the data matrix. The major feature of the model is that a decomposition is sought which simultaneously seeks to locate both the object point locations *and* the category centroids for each subject—this being the degree of individual difference allowed in this model, which thus allows the subject to be represented by a set of category centroids, rather than by a single ideal point, as occurs in unfolding analysis.[51] Because there is a need to begin from the subject-specific data, the matrix notation becomes somewhat complex. I shall therefore oversimplify and refer those interested in the full details to Takane (1980, pp. 76–78).

The intention is to obtain a configuration of stimulus/object points in such a way that the sum of squared intercategory distances (averaged over subjects) is maximized under suitable normalization restrictions. In this process, a significant scaling role is played by the subject-specific similarity matrix, Π_{G_k}, related to the data-matrix G_k by:

$$\Pi_{G_k} = G_k (G_k' G_k)^{-1} G_k'$$

The (j, k) element of $(G_k G_k')$ is 1 when objects j and k are sorted into the same group and is 0 otherwise. The $(G_k' G_k)^{-1}$ matrix scales nonzero elements of $G_k G_k'$ by the size of categories, so that the similarity between two objects sorted into the same group is inversely related to the size of the category (precisely the assumption in Burton's M3).

The purpose of MDSORT is to determine a matrix X of coordinates of the n objects in a minimal, user-chosen dimensionality, r. There is a definitional relation between the squared distances between category centroids and the trace of the product-moment of X:

$$\tfrac{1}{2} tr D^2 = n tr(X'X) = n\left[tr(X'\Pi_{G_k} X) + tr\left(X'\Pi_{G_k}^{\perp} X\right)\right]$$

where

$$\Pi_{G_k}^{\perp} = I_n - \Pi_{G_k}$$

(The second term on the right-hand side represents the sum of squared Euclidean distances between object points and their corresponding category centroids.)

Averaging over subjects, the expression for $tr(X'X)$ can be reduced to:

$$tr(X'BX) + tr(XB^{\perp}X),$$

where

$$B = \frac{1}{N} \sum_{k=1}^{N} \Pi_{G_k}, \qquad B^{\perp} = \frac{1}{N} \sum_{k=1}^{N} \Pi_{G_k}^{\perp}.$$

Takane now chooses to determine X so that $tr(X'BX)$ is maximized for $tr(X'BX) = 1$, and for the multidimensional case we also need the restriction: $X'X = I$. The maximum of $tr(X'BX)$ under this restriction is the matrix of normalized eigenvectors of B corresponding to its r dominant eigenvalues and satisfying the centering requirement by excluding the constant eigenvector. Once X is obtained this way, category centroids for each subject k are given by:

$$Y_k = (G'_k G_k)^{-1} G'_k X$$

and it is these Y_k values that give the information about differences in sorting.

Takane himself points out that however desirable it may be to link the scaling and the representation of the data (e.g., by reproducing aspects of subjects' behavior in making a sorting), this is not actually met in the model (nor, it should be added, in any similar model). The MDSORT solution maximizes the average sum of squared intercluster distances—a useful technical requirement—but it is hardly likely that subjects themselves form their categories so that the sum of the intercategory distances is a maximum.

4.2.3.2. Homogeneity Analysis. Multiple correspondence analysis (Weller and Romney, 1990) is a kind of multivariate extension[52] of simple correspondence analysis from two-way to higher-way tables, and it thus becomes appropriate for sortings data. The original development of multiple correspondence analysis (Benzécri, 1973; Gifi, 1981) was conceived primarily in a graphical context and was designed to take account of all two-way tables that could be formed from the N-way table. However, its geometrical representation has known difficulties of interpretation (Greenacre, 1993; pp. 141–151), and a more straightforward numerical (optimal scaling) form, known as homogeneity analysis, has more often been used.

As in simple correspondence analysis, homogeneity analysis provides optimal scores for the nominal variables of the data. The difference is that the rows and columns of the two-way table now become the objects and the categories of the sorting (as in the sortings PDF data matrix), and the method seeks to provide scores on a prespecified, but small, number of dimensions, which are optimal in the sense that objects sorted into different categories are as far apart as possible, i.e., are maximally discriminated, and those objects most frequently sorted into the same category cluster together, i.e., are homogeneous (hence the name of the procedure).

Homogeneity analysis is implemented as a program in SPSS[53] as HOMALS (homogeneity analysis by alternating least squares) and has the following main characteristics (Gifi, 1981, pp. 101–102):

- Categories and objects are represented as points in a joint space.
- Objects in different categories are maximally separated, and objects in same categories are as close (homogeneous) as possible.
- Category points are the centroid of object points that occur in a given category.
- The distance between object points is related to the similarity of their profiles.
- If a category applies to only one object (a singleton), the object point and the category-point will coincide.

The program provides:

- optimal quantification (scores) of the categories for each variable,
- optimal scores of the objects, and
- discrimination index for each variable (between-category VAF by dimension).

Homogeneity analysis has been used extensively by van der Kloot and his Dutch and Belgian co-researchers to analyze free-sorting data of a number of domains: 281 personality trait adjectives (Van der Kloot and Sloof, 1989), 176 pain-descriptive words (Verkes et al., 1989), and 44 paintings (Van der Kloot, 1996).

A word of caution is in order before embarking on correspondence analysis of partitions data. Hubert and Arabie (1992) have shown that optimal representations of such data are derivable from a one-dimensional correspondence analysis solution and paradoxically that a two-dimensional solution—the usual preference—is derivable from a one-dimensional solution and that a two-dimensional solution is actually less adequate (p. 132).

4.2.3.3. Multidimensional Scalogram Analysis. Sorting data may also be represented by a generalized version of Guttman's scalogram analysis, referred to as multidimensional scalogram analysis (MSA) (Lingoes and Borg, 1978; Zvulun, 1978; Canter, 1983). This is a form of analysis well-adapted to the analysis of free-sorting and used so far primarily in the analysis of multiple sorting and particularly by researchers within the Facet theoretic tradition (Canter, 1985; Borg and Shye, 1995).

In conventional scalogram analysis (Guttman, 1950; Torgerson, 1958), the data consisted of a set of individuals' response patterns created by their pattern of "yes/no" answers to a set of items. If the data satisfy some crucial conditions, then both the rank-order of the items and the rank-order of the individuals/response patterns can be inferred. In the multidimensional analogue, MSA, the data again consist of a set of response patterns (called a "structuple" in MSA terminology), but the constituent items can be polytomous (several categorical alternatives) rather than being simply dichotomous, and a solution is sought in a continuous multidimensional space.

In order to adapt this format to sorting data, some respecification is necessary, and an example is useful.[54] A typical example of data for conventional scalogram analysis is seen in Table 3A: a set of six Inns (six "individuals" or response patterns) is described in terms of three characteristics or "items," the three categorical variables: STYLE, COST, and DISTANCE. Equivalently, in Table 3B the data could be thought of as consisting of three sortings of the six objects (Inns), each sorting corresponding to a different characteristic.

Put in this way, the constituent sortings of a *multiple* sorting can be thought of in the same way as a set of individual sortings. Moreover, it shows that it is straightforward to convert between MSA and PDF formats and terminology: the data matrices are simply transposed versions of each other. What we have called "sortings" are MSA's "items," and our "objects" are MSA's "response patterns" or what Facet theory calls "structuples" (Borg and Shye, 1995).

A MSA solution to sortings data maps the rows, columns, and entries in the data matrix in a distinctive way:

- the *objects* are represented as points,
- each *sorting* is represented as a partition, and
- the *categories* are regions of the partitions.

In terms of output, MSA first produces a master plot (or group space), which portrays the point locations of the objects. Following this are a set of plots, one for each sorting. The objects points are

80

TABLE 3
Example of Coding Sortings for Multidimensional
Scalogram Analysis

A. Conventional Scalogram Format

Six Inns ("individuals") are described in terms of three
characteristics/aspects ["items"]:

STYLE:	Sophisticated (1), Old-world (2), Modern (3), Basic (4)
COST:	Cheap (1), Moderate (2), Expensive (3)
DISTANCE:	Walking (1), Taxi home (2)

The Inns can be described as:

	STYLE	COST	DISTANCE	(Corresponding response pattern or "structuple")		
Inn 1	S	E	T	1	3	2
Inn 2	M	M	T	2	2	2
Inn 3	O	M	W	2	2	1
Inn 4	B	C	W	4	1	1
Inn 5	S	E	W	1	3	1
Inn 6	M	C	T	3	1	1

B. Data in Sortings PDF

	6 objects (= Inns):					
3 sortings:	1	2	2	4	1	3
(= characteristics):	3	2	2	1	3	1
	2	2	1	1	1	1

plotted, but the plot also shows the categories for each sorting. The researcher then sets about determining if there are any clear regions for each category of this first sorting variable. The same is done for each subsequent item plot. All these plots can be laid on top of each other, like transparencies, to show the profile (structuple) for each individual point. A number of applications using the MSA technology to (usually multiple) sorting data are reported for a variety of domains: energy conservation (Wilson and Canter, 1993); prison organization (Canter et al., 1985); landscape judgment (Scott and Canter, 1997); and a further range of applications in Zvulun (1978).

4.3. Three-Way Analysis of Sortings

Quite often, more than one sorting is collected from an individual (see Section 2.6.2), either as a test-retest reliability measure or when different bases of judgment are sought or as a matter of methodological principle (Rosenberg and Kim, 1975; Canter et al., 1985). Alternatively, sortings might be obtained under different experimental conditions, contexts, or times. In each case this will generate data that are natural candidates for three-way analysis (Arabie et al., 1987).

There are two basic forms of three-way sorting data (although there are as yet few instances of their application).

1. *Three-way, three-mode*: a direct scaling of a three-way, three-mode sorting matrix ($N \times p \times c$), where the three distinct ways are individuals $\times$ objects $\times$ multiple criteria/replications/times.
2. *Three-way, two-mode*: a stack of matrices of square proximity measures such as co-occurrences between objects ($p \times p$) or Arabie-Boorman measures between subjects ($N \times N$).

Once again, there are both discrete and spatial models suited to the analysis of these data.

4.3.1. Three-Way, Two-Mode Data: Takane's IDSORT Model

The most directly relevant three-way model is a variant of Takane's MDSORT known as IDSORT (for individual differences sorting; Takane 1981a, 1982a, b), which is much the same as MDSORT, but it additionally makes specific allowance in the model for the representation of *individuals*—not just of their categories. The IDSORT model takes the PDF sortings data matrix as input and proceeds directly to solve for the locations of the objects in the group space (in the user-chosen number of dimensions), and the dimensional weights for each subject, as in the INDSCAL model (Kruskal and Wish, 1978; Arabie et al., 1987).

This is done by applying Carroll and Chang's (1970) canonical decomposition procedure. First the subject-specific similarity matrices Π_{G_k} and aggregated matrix $\Pi_G = \Sigma_k \Pi_{G_k}/N$ are formed (as in MDSORT above), and the similarity matrices are canonically decomposed using the CANDECOMP procedure to provide estimates of:

- the location of the object points in the group space, and
- a set of dimensional weights for each subject.

The *group space* is so named from the INDSCAL model, and it shares the other specific properties of that model. Unlike other

Euclidean spatial models, the orientation of the axes of this space is fixed and may not be rotated without destroying the model's optimal properties. It is by reference to these axes that individual differences are assessed. The group space represents the configuration of a notional subject who weights the dimensions equally and the distances in the group space are weighted Euclidean.

Each individual's dimensional weight can be interpreted as the importance she attaches to a given dimension in judgments she makes about the objects. However, once an individual's dimensional weights are applied to the group space, this produces a new systematically distorted ("private") space, *within* which the distances are Euclidean, but in comparison between subjects their spaces have to be differentially weighted, and the form of the model is thus a weighted Euclidean distance model (Carroll and Chang, 1970).

Subjects' patterns of weights are depicted as points—strictly, vector ends from the origin—plotted in the same dimensions, to form the subject space. If subjects' patterns of weights are to be compared this must be in terms of their *angular separation* of their vectors and *not* in terms of their (apparent) distance in the subject space.[55] Various devices (such as Young's "weirdness index" and "flattened weights" in SPSS; Norušis, 1994, pp. 207–212) have been developed to ensure the correct interpretation of such weights; the same issues apply to Takane's IDSORT weights.

Finally, from the CANDECOMP solution there can be derived both the subject category centroids (as in MDSORT) in the group space and, in principle, the category centroids in the subject's private space.

4.3.2. Other Models

Many of the other models that could be applied to sorting data are of largely academic interest in the sense that their use has been sparse. However, many of them have considerable potential relevance and therefore need a brief outline.

4.3.2.1. Symmetrical INDSCAL. If a set of co-occurrence measures (or, indeed a set of partition measures) has been calculated, these can readily be represented by a variant of individual differences scaling, sometimes known as S-INDSCAL (symmetric individual differences scaling), so named because the input matrices are symmetric). In this case, each measure is a "pseudo-subject," i.e., considered as if it were a subject in its own right, and the behavior of the measures in representing the sorting data is compared by looking at the pattern of dimensional weights. The same considerations apply here as in any other INDSCAL-based weighted Euclidean distance model.

4.3.2.2. Procrustean Analysis. An alternative approach to comparing the configurations is to use Procrustean analysis, where each matrix is separately scaled, and the resulting *configurations* are then input as data to a Procrustean individual differences scaling (PINDIS) program.[56] This procedure first rotates the configurations into maximum conformity, using permissible similarity transformations—reflection, rigid rotation, and uniform re-scaling—to produce a reference centroid configuration. This forms the basic configuration to which a hierarchy of individual differences models of increasingly more complex form are fitted to obtain greater conformity of each individual configuration to the centroid configuration. In a sense the PINDIS hierarchy of models attempts to answer questions about the type and degree of complexity necessary to account for differences between various data sources, measures, and models.

4.3.2.3. Three-Way Additive Clustering. Just as MDSORT generalizes naturally to its three-way version IDSORT, so the additive clustering model ADCLUS generalizes to INDCLUS (individual differences clustering) (Carroll and Arabie, 1983; Arabie et al., 1987), implemented using a variant of the MAPCLUS algorithm (Arabie and Carroll, 1980a). As in the INDSCAL model, three-way, two-mode data are assumed for this model, so it is well adapted to the analysis of a stack of proximity measures, especially between objects. The form of the model is:

$$s_{ij}^h \approx \sum_k w_{hk} p_{ik} p_{jk} + c_h$$

where $p_{ik} = 1$ if object i is in cluster k and is 0 otherwise, $p_{jk} = 1$ if object j is in cluster k and is 0 otherwise, w_{hk} is the (non-negative) weight for subject h on cluster k, and c_h is the additive constant for subject h.

The difference between this and the ADCLUS model is the individual cluster-weight value (and the additive, "universal-set" constant) The individual weight is specific to the "subject" (in the current case of sorting data, the individual measure or replication), but the presence/absence parameters are common to all. Once again, this model is analogous to the INDSCAL model, but where discrete cluster membership is the structure rather than a continuous space. An extended example of the application of INDCLUS to Rosenberg and Kim's (1975) multiple sorting studies of kinship terms is presented in the next section.

Finally, there are a range of other three-way models that could, in principle, be applied to sortings data, but which are unlikely to be suitable either because the constraints imposed by sortings data on the solution are too few or weak to produce a stable solution or because the models concerned make assumptions that are unlikely to be met for sortings data:

- INDTREE (Carroll et al., 1984), discussed in Corter (1996).
- Three-mode factor analysis, developed initially by Tucker (1964), of which the most stable version and one that solves the indeterminacy of factor rotation in much the same way as CANDECOMP is Harshman et al.'s (1984) PARAFAC model.

4.4. Applications

In this final section, both general and specific examples of sorting methodology are given. First, a range of applications of sorting methodology are summarized in Table 4. The table makes no claim to be either exhaustive or representative, but comments are in order, and several trends are evident.

- Early sorting studies were almost entirely in psycholinguistics, but now increasingly come from other areas in psychology. Subsequent studies came from anthropology and later from other social sciences.
- The subjects for sorting are drawn predominantly from university students.
- The number of objects used in sorting varies very widely, but there seems to be a feasible lower limit around 30 and a surprisingly high maximum of 281.

TABLE 4
Illustrative Applications of Sorting Methodology

Domain	Subjects	Objects	Variant	Measure / Direct	Model	Comment	Reference
		Data					
1. Animal/plants							
a. Monkeys (sociometric)	Nights	16 vervet monkeys	Free/multiple	PAIRBONDS (D)	MDS	Time-series (cohort)	Arabie and Boorman, 1973; Struhsaker, 1967
b. Fish: shapes	15 novice 4 × 15 expert	43 fish line drawings	Free	Co-occurrence (M1)	MDS, optimal scaling	Names and drawings	Boster and Johnson, 1989
c. Dogs	102 M/F dog owners	39 problem situations with dogs	Free (3–15 groups)	n/s (similarity)	MDS, HCS (average-link)	Pretest	Ben-Michael et al., 1997
d. Plant, animal names	n.s.	"Several"	Free	n.s.	n.s.	"Group with one another"	Berlin et al., 1968
2. Health							
a. Pain	53 students	176 (Dutch) pain words	Free	Direct	HOMALS, centroid cluster		Verkes et al., 1989
b. IV drugs	5 dermatologists	282 skin lesions of drug users	Free	n/a	n/a		Cagle et al., 1998
c. Psychiatry	25 students	89 reasons for visiting psychiatrist	Free/multiple	Rosenberg δ	MDS, HCS		Rosenberg and Cohen, 1977
d.	11 staff	96 items (views on patient program)	Free	Co-occurrence	MDS, HCS		Trochim, 1989
e. Risk	11 and 17 young Navaho men	43 risks (6 subtypes)	Free	Co-occurrence	MDS, HCS	Pre- and posttest intervention	Trotter and Potter, 1993
f. Ward layout	25 staff	24 patients 40 activities	Multiple	Direct	MSA		Canter and King, 1996
g. Disability classification	450 health workers; disabled, carers	90 activities	Free	Co-occurrence	HCS, MDS, factor	International study	Trotter et al., 1997
3. Kinship							
a. Kinship	170 M/F students	15 kin terms	Free/single	Rosenberg δ	INDSCAL, HCS	Classic multiple	Rosenberg and Kim, 1975
	160 M/F (multiple)		Free/multiple	Direct Triple co-occurrence	INDCLUS MDS, HCS	In text	Carroll and Arabie, 1983 Daws, 1996

(continued)

TABLE 4
Illustrative Applications of Sorting Methodology (continued)

Domain	Subjects	Objects	Data Variant	Measure / Direct	Model	Comment	Reference
b. Marriage rules	200 students	56 descriptions and photos	Fixed (2); successive	Contingency	Fuzzy logic inference		Nave, 1998
4. Occupations							
a. Occupational titles	54 students	60 occupations	Free	Co-occurrence (M4)	MDS, HCS		Burton, 1972
b. Occupational titles, descriptions	71	32 names	Free	Co-occurrence	MDS, HCS	Joint scaling	Coxon and Jones, 1979a, b
	66 (Sample)	50 descrs.	Free	(3 variants)	MDSORT IDSORT		Coxon et al., 1986
c. Theologians	48 students	19 professors	Free	Co-occurrence	MDS		Sorenson, 1997
5. Perception							
a. Colors	21 "young adults".	6 color chips	Free and successive division	Ultrametric dissimilarity	HCS		Boster, 1986
	32 students	8 color terms					
b. Dots	24 students	48 dots; 112 predefined patterns	Discriminability				Imai, 1966; Imai and Garner, 1968
c. Facial expressions	70	5 schematic faces	Free	MLE direct	Response scaling		Hojo, 1986
d.	22 "observers" (students)	72 face-photos (Frois-Wittmann)	Free	Co-occurrence	None reported	Earliest instance?	Hulin and Katz, 1935
e. Emotions	20 adults	30 facial photographs	Free-sort and hierarchy	Co-occurrence	MLE/MDS		Bimler and Kirkland, 1997
f. Personality traits	69 students	60 traits	Free	Profile distance	MDS, HCS	Early example	Rosenberg et al., 1968; Rosenberg and Jones, 1972
	25 students	50 traits	Free	Co-occurrence and Rosenberg δ	HOMALS, MDS	Comparison of proximity measures	van der Kloot and van Herk, 1991
	42 students	60 traits	Overlapping	Rosenberg δ	MDS		Wing and Nelson, 1972
	45 students	281 adjectives	Free	Direct	HOMALS		van der Kloot and Sloof, 1989

				Direct	HOMALS		
6. Politics/power							
a. Power strategies	25 students	16 strategies	Free				van der Kloot and Sloof, 1989
b. Voting	Candidates	Voters	Derived	n-tuple; Jaccard	MDS	Classic n-tuples	Cox et al., 1991
c. Journalism	40 students	76 editorial statements about race riots	Free and rank	Rosenberg δ	MDS, HCS		Schmidt, 1972
d. Nations	75 students	21 nations	Free and multiple	Co-occurrence	MDS, INDSCAL		Wish and Carroll, 1974
e. Sexual harassment	34 students	50 photos + 143 adjectives + 18 scenarios	Free	Mean distance	MDS		Rhodes and Stern, 1994
7. Verbal behavior							
a.	4 × 24 M/F children	36 words	Free	Co-occurrence	MDS, HCS	Classic study	Anglin, 1970
b.	5 × 40 M/F children to adults	20 words	Free	Co-occurrence	MDS, HCS		Anglin (in Miller, 1967)
c.	4 × 40	20 words	Fixed (4)	Co-occurrence	MDS, HCS	Also "reject" pile	
d.	41 M/F students	i. 29 propositions	Free	Co-occurrence	MDS, HCS		Fillenbaum and Rapoport, 1972
		ii. 29 HAVE words			MDSORT		Rapoport and Fillenbaum, 1971
		iii. 40 good/bad words					Takane, 1980
e.	50 students	48 nouns	Free	Co-occurrence	HCS	Classic Definitions of Burton measures	Miller 1967, 1969
f.	50 students	34 behaviors verbs	Free	Co-occurrence (3 variants)	MDS		Burton, 1975
8. Miscellaneous							
a. Socioeconomic environment	Residents in 8 communities	20/24 place qualities	Free, Likert	Co-occurrence	MDS, HCS, consensus	Extensive community study (North Carolina)	Maiolo et al., 1993
b. Photographic scenes	High school students	10 photos	Multiple, free	Co-occurrence (M1 and M4)	Multiscale		Donderi, 1988
c. Casinos	1 gambler	8 casinos	Multiple	Individual	MSA		Canter et al., 1985

- The number of objects usually outnumbers the number of people doing the sorting.
- The great majority of reported studies use *free*-sorting [but Q methodology, relying on fixed number of categories, forced distributions, and ranked categories represents an important variant, but one largely covered elsewhere (McKeown and Thomas, 1988)]. The Rosenberg injunction to use multiple sorts tends to have been heeded most within that same tradition and also in the Facet theoretic traditions (Canter, 1985). Very few instances have been found of researchers deliberately permitting multiple allocation to categories.
- If sorting data are scaled directly (joint solutions), they have been analyzed primarily with the Takane models, but increasingly SPSS/HOMALS is being used.
- If data are interpreted as one-mode, the measures used are almost entirely of *object* similarity rather than individual partition similarity. The measures chosen concentrate almost exclusively on co-occurrence —whether direct frequencies (usually unweighted) or extended frequencies (such as the δ measure within the Rosenberg tradition).
- By far the most common forms of models for analysis of two-way, one-mode sorting data has been multidimensional scaling and Johnson's hierarchical clustering schemes, and both are normally the nonmetric variants.

Example 1: Reanalysis of Rosenberg Kinship Data

A recent study deserves extended attention as an example of the way in which analysis of sortings is developing. It consists of the application of INDCLUS to the multiple sorting data of Rosenberg and Kim (1975)[57] by Carroll and Arabie (1983, pp. 525–528). The data and other relevant aspects of the analysis are also contained in Arabie et al. (1987, pp. 57–64).

In the Rosenberg study, 85 male and 85 female subjects were instructed to make a (single) free-sorting of 15 kinship terms. A further 80 male and 80 female subjects were instructed to make *more than one* free-sorting of the kinship terms, using a different basis for each. (Only the first two examples of sortings were analyzed by Carroll and Arabie.) In all, this specifies six conditions:

1. M1: male-single sort,
2. F1: female-single sort;
3. M1st: male-first sorting,

4. M2nd: male-second sorting;
5. F1st: female-first sorting,
6. F2nd: female-second sorting.

The sorting data were aggregated for each of these six conditions to form a lower-triangular matrix of co-occurrences [using Miller (1969) and Burton's F similarity measure, M1], and the six matrices were input into INDCLUS, with a prespecified number of five clusters or categories.[58] The solution obtained by Carroll and Arabie (1984) is presented in Figure 16.

Rosenberg and Kim mention two bases used to structure kinship terms: (1) by generation and (2) by gender. The solution reproduced in Figure 16 (with an excellent goodness of fit) presents:

- the set of "subject weights" for each of the six conditions,
- the specification of the kin terms making up the cluster to which the weight refers, and
- a brief interpretation.

The solution is simple to interpret, and the differences in the patterns of weights are also interesting. Rosenberg's assertion that single sortings tend to ignore "obvious" characteristics—in this case, gender—is reflected in the relatively small weights for the two single-sort conditions. Carroll and Arabie (1983, p. 527) go on to comment:

> For the multiple-sort conditions, it is interesting to note that female subjects emphasized sex in the first sorting (given that the two relevant clusters have much higher weights), whereas male subjects waited until the second sorting to emphasize the salience of sex as a factor in sorting kinship terms. Across all conditions, females' data were better fitted to the model than were males' data. Also, data from the first sort were better fitted than for the second sort, for both males and females.

Occupations Data. Following the analysis reported above in Section 3.4, the Arabie-Boorman partition measures for individual occupational sortings were first calculated and scaled in two dimensions. The Burton co-occurrence measures were also calculated and scaled, initially using multidimensional scaling and hierarchical clustering and subsequently using Takane's MDSORT and IDSORT.[59]

INDCLUS Category Weights: Sex/Sorting-Type Condition (for each of 6 subjects = conditions)*

	F1 (1)	M1 (2)	F1st (3)	F2nd (4)	M1st (5)	M2nd (6)	Cluster and Composition	Interpretation
A	.052	.143	.551	.241	.299	.295	A: brother, father, grandfather	Male relatives, excluding cousin, grandson, nephew, son, uncle
B	.049	.146	.554	.246	.291	.306	B: aunt, daughter, granddaughter, grandmother, mother, niece, sister	Female relatives, excluding cousin
C	.552	.397	.283	.373	.340	.237	C: aunt, cousin, nephew, niece, uncle	Collateral relations
D	.478	.372	.206	.372	.241	.219	D: brother, daughter, father, mother, sister, son	Nuclear family
E	.626	.449	.251	.385	.395	.253	E: granddaughter, grandfather, grandmother, grandson	Direct ancestors, descendants ±2 generations
Additive constants	.055	.075	.132	.158	.158	.207	Additive constants	
Variance accounted for	78.6	68.8	96.3	78.9	82.4	71.7	Variance accounted for	(Overall VAF = 81.1%)

Figure 16. INDCLUS analysis of Rosenberg and Kim's six sets of sortings data. * F1, female-first sorting; M1, male-single sort; F1st, female-first sorting; F2nd, female-second sorting; M1st, male-first sorting; M2nd male-second sorting. (Data from Rosenberg and Kim, 1975; analysis from Carroll and Arabie, 1983.)

91

Individual Sorting. The two-dimensional configuration for the PAIRBONDS (*D*) measure, scaled using MINISSA, a nonmetric Euclidean distance model, is shown in Figure 17. The stress₁ $(\hat{d})$ values indicated an acceptable two-dimensional solution.[60]

Each of the 71 sortings is represented as a point, and most of the points are labeled with a value that indicates their height value. The scaling behavior of these measures, described by Arabie and Boor-

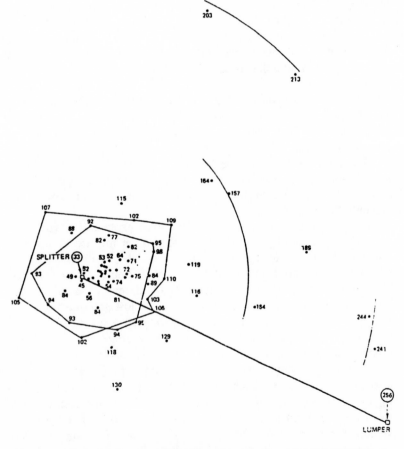

Figure 17. Occupations data: two-dimensional scaling of PAIRBONDS distances between sortings of occupational titles.

man as concentric circles of equal height value, is clearly discernible in this solution. The highest height value (of an Episcopalian priest) acts as surrogate for the lumper and a Post-Office Clerk similarly acted as the splitter, and their points are joined to form the lumper-splitter axis. Because the sortings are only a very small fraction of the possible partitions of 32 objects (occupational titles), we should not expect an easily discernible structure of concentric circles, but it is easy to recognize when the points with similar height values are connected. (The structure around the splitter is fairly confused because a lot of points congregate there.) Those subjects prone to lumping are drawn somewhat unrepresentatively from professional occupations, but such structural characteristics of sorting do not seem to be associated systematically with occupational membership, and, if anything, working class subjects are least prone to produce few, strongly demarked, classes of occupations.

Co-Occurrence of Objects. The individual data were also converted into co-occurrence matrices and aggregated according to Burton's four measures. They, too were nonmetrically scaled in 5-1 dimensions. Once again, the stress$_1$ $(\hat{d})$ values compare favorably with the simulated random values (see Section 4.2.2 and Figure 15 above). The two-dimensional solutions, put into maximum conformity with each other by generalized Procrustes rotation (Gower, 1975), are presented in Figure 18.

The contours imposed on the solution need explanation. The same data were analyzed by hierarchical clustering, giving rise to a single-link and complete linkage dendrograms, which are identical in the first five levels and very similar from that point. Requiring that clusters be based upon the judgments of at least one-half of the number of subjects and that the number of clusters conform to the average number of categories formed produces a cut-off level of 35 (out of 71), and the hierarchical clustering scheme at this level—a crude consensus classification—is mapped into the configuration. Because the subjects have given verbal descriptions of their categories, it is possible to match the clusters by the subjects' corresponding categories and examine the descriptions which they give. Reading from the top right-hand corner in a clockwise direction gives Unskilled, Working Class, Artists, Professions, and "Dealing with People," as the common, brief, appellations for the main clusters (Coxon and Jones, 1979a, pp. 42–43).

93

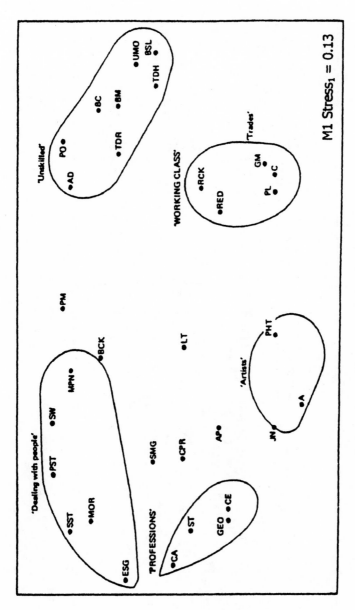

Figure 18. Scaling of co-occurrence of 32 occupations (Burton's four measures).

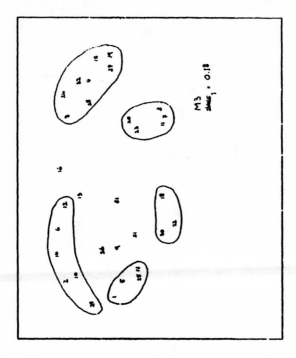

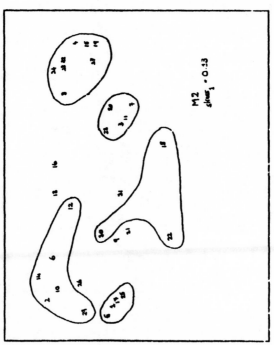

Figure 18. (continued)

1 Chartered Accountant	CA	17 Civil Engineer	CE
2 Secondary School Teacher	SST	18 Photographer	PHT
3 Garage Mechanic	GM	19 Building Site Labourer	BSL
4 Barman	BM	20 Restaurant Cook	RCK
5 Statistician	ST	21 Airline Pilot	AP
6 Social Worker	SW	22 Actor	A
7 Carpenter	C	23 Railway Engine Driver	RED
8 Ambulance Driver	AD	24 Postman	PO
9 Computer Programmer	CPR	25 Geologist	GEO
10 Minister of Religion	MOR	26 Sales Manager	SMG
11 Plumber	PL	27 Trawler Deckhand	TDH
12 Male Psychiatric Nurse	MPN	28 Taxi driver	TDR
13 Bank Clerk	BCK	29 Eye Surgeon	ESG
14 Primary School Teacher	PST	30 Journalist	JN
15 Machine Operator	UMO	31 Laboratory Tech.	LT
16 Policeman	PM	32 Bus Conductor	BCR

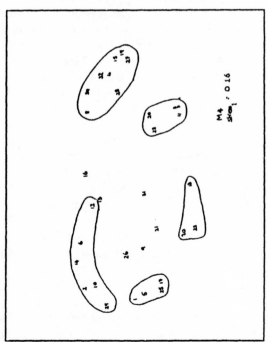

Figure 18. (continued)

96

If the recovery of structure from the sorting task depends upon differential discrimination, then we may expect to find significant differences in the MDS solutions. In any event, the similarity of the maps produced from scaling the four distance measures is striking. As may be expected, M3 and M4 solutions are very similar indeed, since they both exaggerate fine discriminations. The only nontrivial differences in location between the best- and worst-fitting solutions occur for two occupations: *Journalist* (close to the "Professions" group for M2 and within the "Artists" group in others) and *Sales Manager* (close to the "Professions" group in M2). Perhaps the most striking feature of the solution is what might facetiously be termed "le triage dichotomique": the first dimension separates out two main clusters—"professional" versus "working class" in the subjects' terminology—which are in turn differentiated into people-oriented/extrinsic reward and skilled/unskilled subgroups; the "artists" group is simply incongruous with the others.

Finally, the same co-occurrence data were scaled using the Takane programs, and the first two dimensions of the three-dimensional IDSORT stimulus configuration is given in Figure 19. Since this model is seeking to accommodate and represent individual differences in sorting and is a direct solution rather than one mediated via a measure of proximity, it is not surprising that the pattern of point locations is rather different compared to Figure 18. Again, it is readily interpretable—this time at a dimensional level, since as we have seen, all INDSCAL-like models have fixed reference dimensions for the subject weights. The first dimension separates the Professions and the Working Class groups. The most interesting new structure occurs in the second dimensions with the working class occupations laid out almost as a straight line. A puzzling feature is that the middle-class occupations seem to be arrayed in the opposite direction of skill, and they are far less discriminated. The third dimension simply separates the "Artists" group from the other occupations. Quite clearly, this solution represents the disjunction of Professions and Working Class occupations, and the unravelling of the Working Class group into an unmistakable linear scale of relative skill.

4.5. Summary

The method of free-sorting, despite its apparent lack of structure, turns out to be an interesting task for subjects, is usable with large

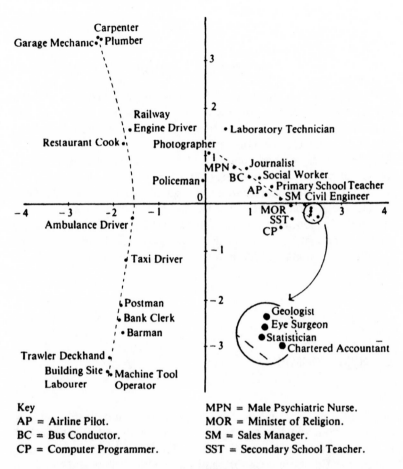

Figure 19. IDSORT scaling of 32 occupational titles.

number of objects, and now possesses a methodology for the representation and analysis of the data, which is as extensive as any other method of data collection. It can be adapted to survey contexts, and there is a wide variety of nominal data that can be thus interpreted. The advent of computer-aided data collection and expert systems makes its use even more straightforward, and the development of two- and three-way variants of spatial models and discrete representations make free-sorting an even more attractive proposition.

ABOUT THE AUTHOR

A. P. M. COXON is Professor of Sociology at the University of Essex and Emeritus Professor of Sociological Research Methods of the University of Wales. Previous appointments have been at Leeds, Edinburgh, and Cardiff Universities and a visiting professorship at MIT. His other methodological research interests include multidimensional scaling, sexual diaries, and qualitative data analysis, together with substantive research interests in sexual health and behavior and social stratification. He has published over 50 articles in a wide range of journals and disciplines, and his books, which have a sorting component, include a trilogy on occupational cognition, a text on multidimensional scaling and a recent book on sexual diaries.

ACKNOWLEDGMENTS

My thanks are first due to Mary MacPherson and Ruth Lockhart, who undertook our first sorting experiments with real people (as well as students) and wrote up their experiences and also to the many students at Edinburgh, Cardiff, and Essex Universities and the Essex Summer School who helped nurture this work to fruition through its various versions (and especially to Lynn Pettinger who commented in detail on the text).

Especial thanks are due to Phipps Arabie, whose work and advice are so evident here, as also to Kim Romney, Mike Burton, John Kirkland and Dave Bimler, David Canter, Henry Cagle, Robert T. Trotter, and Willem Van der Kloot who in many differing ways have helped with information, advice, or evaluation.

Finally, thanks are due to Michael Lewis-Beck whose editorial assistance and encouragement through some dark days were invaluable and to my partner Phil Hawkins who has helped keep the show on the road and assisted in so many ways.